Protecting Your Family in Dangerous Times

BY
KELLIE COPELAND

KENNETH
COPELAND
PUBLICATIONS

Protecting Your Family in Dangerous Times

ISBN 978-1-57562-971-1   30-7787

18 17 16 15 14 13   15 14 13 12 11 10

© 2002 Kellie Copeland

Kenneth Copeland Publications
Fort Worth, TX 76192-0001

For more information about Kenneth Copeland Ministries, visit kcm.org or call 1-800-600-7395 (U.S. only) or +1-817-852-6000.

This book is dedicated to my children:
Rachel, Caleb, Lyndsey, Jenny, Max and Emily

Acknowledgments

Thank you, Rachel, Caleb, Lyndsey, Jenny, Max and Emily—for being all that a mother could dream of in her children. Thank you for being obedient and pleading the blood of Jesus every day.

Thank you, Mother and Daddy, for teaching me the Word and living a life of faith before me. Because of you, I trust in God.

And, to the rest of my family, thank you for your support, your prayer and for believing in me.

A special thank you to my pastors—Terri and George—for everything.

And to Billye Brim, I give a hearty thank you! I'm grateful to you for starting me on this journey and teaching me about the blood of Jesus.

Thank you also to Jerry and Carolyn Savelle for being there every time I need you.

Most of all, thank You, Jesus, for Your precious blood and thank You for seeing to it that I don't miss out on anything You have for me.

Love and thanks to all,

Kellie Copeland

Contents

Acknowledgments

Foreword

Introduction

1. Make Sure Your Children Are
   Fully Protected 1

2. Applying the Blood: From Passover
   to Present 13

3. Protection Through God's Grace 37

4. Our Sanctuary—The Holy of Holies 51

5. The Absolute Certainty of Divine Protection 73

6. It's Your Choice! 97

7. It Matters Where You Live 123

Prayer of Protection for Your Family

Contents

Foreword

by Kenneth Copeland

The shed blood of Jesus is the fullness of love expressed, holding out its offer of salvation to the extreme—divine protection from sin, sickness, demons, fear and hell. It is heaven's guarantee on the earth that all God has promised is divinely true. True to any and all who will accept it so that all may walk in its glorious protection and holy prosperity. Think about it. The spotless, pure, sinless, holy, righteous blood of Almighty God—Love Himself— poured out for the likes of you and me! Read this book, thinking about it. Read a couple of chapters and then stop and meditate on it again.

This is a very important book for this dangerous hour in which we live. Read it until fear is flushed out of your life like a covey of birds flushed out of their hiding places and rushing away before your face. God loves you! He poured out His life for you. He swore every promise of His holy Word directly to you in His own blood on the Cross. Receive it. Take your place as His very own love child. Cry out of your heart from the spirit of adoption—"I have a Father! He's mine and I'm His! He is The Most High God and He's my Father. I know Him and He knows me. I have it in writing in His own blood. There is no greater love than the way He loves me."

The Spirit of God has inspired Kellie to bring this message to us and has anointed her to share parts of her life with us. Read it and live it with her as you read.

May God richly bless and keep you.

JESUS IS LORD!

Kenneth Copeland

Introduction

God is so gracious to give us exactly what we need, just when we need it. I believe this book is one of those gifts. I know when He began to reveal these things to me, that was exactly how I felt. I knew I had been given a precious gift—a deeper understanding of the protection of the blood of Jesus.

As I began my final edits on this book, the world and America as we knew it were changed in one tragic moment on September 11, 2001. It was more than just an attack on our nation—it was a direct assault on God and on His people. I began to realize that God wants people to know we can trust Him with our whole lives, and more importantly, with our families.

As I prayed about whether or not to add things into this book concerning war, terrorism and biological threats, I felt the Lord wanted me to leave it the way He had given it to me. He knew what we would face in these days and has everything we need to see us through. Praise God, even though the world may change, God's Word will not. He wants us to lay hold of all He has for us and go forward in victory over the enemy!

A final thought before you begin reading this book: In reflecting on the changes in our lives since we began to plead the blood of Jesus, I realized that fear had been eradicated from our family. The blood of Jesus has wiped it out!

Do you realize that in any battle you face, fear will cause you to lose? In fear, we say the wrong things and do the wrong things. But when we begin to plead the blood of Jesus, faith is built up and fear loses its grip on us. In the absence of fear, we make the right decisions and speak the Word of God. Victory is ours!

I am very thankful to my Jesus, not only for His blood, but also for opening my eyes to real life in Him.

Kellie Copeland

CHAPTER 1

Make Sure Your Children Are Fully Protected

As a parent, you probably know only too well the overriding desire to protect your children from harm. You deal with that desire every time you send them out the door to school or watch your teenagers drive off with their friends to the mall or to a movie.

But what goes through your mind in those moments when your children leave home for another day's activities? Just how sure are you that God will bring them home safely? Do you know with absolute confidence that the blood of Jesus will protect and deliver your children from every danger the world can throw at them that day?

Developing that rock-solid confidence is the goal you should be aiming at as a parent. But how do you reach that goal? What can you do to ensure your children are protected every moment of every day?

A Wake-Up Call

I really began seeking the Lord about how to protect my children after my cousin Nikki died in a car accident. Nikki was Miss "On Fire for God." She was one of the most phenomenal people I have ever known. She had gone to Bible school in Sweden and was about the boldest thing on two feet you have ever seen!

Nikki didn't mince any words with people. She was very bold about speaking out her faith—a real powerhouse for God.

But Nikki's life was suddenly snuffed out. The day before one of our Southwest Believers' Conventions, she was killed in a car accident involving a drunk driver.

Nikki's death was a huge wake-up call to me. I would never question God by saying, "Why did You let this happen?" I did, however, pray, "Lord, I want You to show me how we let this happen. What do we need to do to make sure it never happens again?"

God began to answer that prayer immediately. The same week Nikki died, a close friend and anointed minister named Billye Brim, who teaches on the blood of Jesus, stressed to me that, "We have to plead the blood of Jesus over our families every morning and every night."

It was the first time I had heard we needed to do that. It was such a profound revelation to me! I thought, *I don't know what she's talking about—but I'm going to find out!* (Billye has written a wonderful book on this subject I recommend to everyone, called *The Blood and the Glory.*)

From that time on, I began pleading the blood of Jesus over my children every day, just because Billye told me to. Later she came to our church and taught us more in depth about the blood of Jesus. As I began to walk in what I learned, the Lord began to teach me more.

You see, I'm the type of person who likes to know *why* things work. So I began to study the Word on the subject. Once I learned more about the power in the blood of Jesus, I didn't need anyone else to prompt me. I determined to daily claim the protection of the blood of Jesus over myself, my family and my children for the rest of my life! It took some time to build it into a habit and lifestyle, but once I understood why I needed to plead the blood, it was easy to make the decision to do it.

I'm so grateful to the Lord for opening my eyes to His protection. And, as trouble escalates in the world, I realize more and more what a priceless gift God has given me. As my children go about their daily activities, I know with absolute certainty they will be safe. As they get into their cars and drive off, I know that, no matter what, they are protected and will arrive home safely.

What a gift that is! And the wonderful thing is that you don't have to take as long as I did to enjoy that gift. You can begin operating in the truths presented in this book today!

Take Advantage of Angelic Protection

Pleading the blood of Jesus is the main thing God taught me pertaining to divine protection after Nikki's death. However, before I go on to share other things He taught me about the blood of Jesus, I want to mention three truths He taught me that must be operating in your life if your children are to be fully protected. I want to make sure every area of your life is covered according to the Word of God.

First, you have to understand and appropriate the angelic ministry. Angels are servants sent to minister for you. The world has made them little gods or icons, but the truth is, they are servants. More importantly, they are *your* servants.

According to Hebrews 2:5-6 AMP, angels are not placed higher than you spiritually:

> For it was not to angels that God subjected the habitable world of the future, of which we are speaking. It has been solemnly and earnestly said in a certain place, What is man that You are mindful of him, or the son of man that You

graciously and helpfully care for and visit and
look after him?

We may seem insignificant when we compare ourselves
to angels. But God doesn't see it that way. He sent His angels
to helpfully care for and look after us!

Hebrews 1:14 says, "Are they not all ministering spirits,
sent forth to minister for them who shall be heirs of salvation?" "Them" in that verse is talking about us. We are the
heirs of salvation, and the angels have been sent to minister
for us! That means we have been given the authority to tell
the angels what to do, according to the Word of God.

Therefore, you need to understand how to send your
angels about their business of ministering for you. You also
need to understand how not to mess up what they are trying
to do for you with careless words of doubt and unbelief!

I once read a book by Charles Capps entitled *Angels:
Knowing Their Purpose, Releasing Their Power* that greatly
helped me. I grew up learning how to speak the Word and
avoid speaking negative things, but this book made me pay
even more attention to my words than I had before.

Charles Capps' book will cause you to restrain your lips
from speaking negatively—to just be quiet, if that's what it
takes. It will also teach you how to begin speaking right
things so your angels can do what they need to do for you.

For example, suppose you keep telling your child, "Don't go out in the street, or a car will hit you." An opportunity may never arise in your child's life to run out in the street at the same time a car is driving past, but if that situation ever did arise, the angels would only be able to act according to the words of your mouth.

According to what you've been saying, your will is that the approaching car would hit your child, who should have heeded your words and stayed out of the street. Thus, your angels have to fold their hands. They can't rescue your child or keep the car from hitting him because you have been saying, "Don't go out in the street, or *a car will hit you.*"

God has given you the authority to command the angels to act on your behalf. Therefore, it is very important you watch what comes out of your mouth. Make sure your words reflect what you want to come to pass because your angels were created to obey what you say. *Prayer Point*

So charge the angels to go forth on your behalf. Say, "I charge you, angels, in the Name of Jesus, to watch over my children today, to go before them to protect them and keep them from all harm!" Then make sure you don't speak any negative words that bind their hands from helping you!

Listen to Your Spirit

Another thing the Lord dealt with me about after Nikki

died is that you have to learn to listen to your spirit. This is so important. You can't protect your children if you haven't learned to discern what the Spirit of God is saying to you. (Two of the best books to help you along this line are entitled *To Know Him* and *Hearing From Heaven*, both written by my mother, Gloria Copeland, who is well-skilled in listening to her own spirit.)

You see, God is always speaking to us. I don't believe one calamity ever happens to us that the Holy Spirit didn't speak to our spirits beforehand to warn us.

John 16:13 says the Spirit of truth will show us things to come. He knows what the enemy is trying to do. But we have to learn to pick up on what He is saying so we can obey Him. If we are in tune to His voice, He can protect us from the devil's attacks on our lives.

There have certainly been times in my life when I have failed to heed the Holy Spirit's warning. When certain negative things have happened to me or my family, I've been able to look back and see that the Holy Spirit nudged me to go a different way or to do something I didn't do.

I finally prayed, "Lord, I want to learn how to hear Your voice. I want to know exactly what Your voice sounds like so when You are speaking to me, I will pick up on it." I'm telling you, God took me to school after I prayed that prayer! He put me through one little exercise after another, and His training caused me to grow light years in my spiritual walk!

If you've never prayed that prayer, I strongly suggest you do it. All you have to do is say, "Lord, I want to be able to hear You when You speak to me. I want to know what You sound like."

I promise you, God will answer that prayer and start teaching you through simple little lessons. During the day, you'll hear something on the inside and you'll think, *Was that God?* Then after you either act on His prompting or ignore it, He'll come right behind it and prove to you that it *was* His voice you heard. As Isaiah 30:21 AMP says, "Your ears will hear a word behind you, saying, This is the way; walk in it."

How can you be sure God will teach you how to hear what He is saying to you? Proverbs 3:5-6 tells you: "Trust in the Lord with all thine heart; and lean not unto thine own understanding. In all thy ways acknowledge him, and he shall direct thy paths." When you ask the Lord to teach you how to discern His voice, you are acknowledging He knows more than you do. And because you are acknowledging Him, He will begin to direct your paths.

First Peter 5:8 tells you to be sober and vigilant. That is also part of listening to the Spirit of God. Keep your spiritual antenna up, always listening on the inside for the Holy Spirit's leading. Stay vigilant to plead the blood of Jesus over your children and to pray for them every day.

Be ever watchful because the enemy walks about as a roaring lion, seeking whom he may devour. But as you listen to your spirit and heed the Holy Spirit's voice, you can make sure he never has the opportunity to devour you or your family!

Discipline Your Children

I want to point out one more thing the Lord taught me when I asked Him to show me how to keep my children protected. He told me, *If you want your children to be protected, you will have to discipline them.*

There's no way around it. The Word says if your children are going to live long on the earth, they have to obey their parents (Ephesians 6:1-3). That doesn't just happen automatically. You have to teach them to be obedient, and the only way to do that is to discipline them.

You know, *discipline* is an ugly word to many people in today's society. Sadly, many Christians have bought into the world's idea of discipline.

The world says if you discipline your children, they are going to turn against you and hate you. But actually, the exact opposite is true.

God laid out the perfect system in His Word for disciplining your children. Interestingly, He doesn't even mention "timeouts"! Actually, the only form of parental discipline the Word really talks about is spanking—and that's the one kind of discipline the world says not to use! Interesting, huh? (I recommend you read the now out-of-print book by Chuck Sturgeon called *Train Up Your Child*.[1] It is an excellent book on how to scripturally discipline your children.)

What amazes me is that so many believers have agreed with the world on this subject of discipline. They say, "Well, the Bible is outdated in its instructions on discipline. Spanking a child is too violent." Not surprisingly, these Christians are also reaping the same results in their children that the world does—disobedience, disrespect and rebellion!

I haven't found any truth in the Bible that has passed away—and that includes God's instructions on parental discipline. It's important we learn to discipline our children God's way.

Some people say, "Well, I am praying that my children will be obedient and not stray from the Word; therefore, I don't have to spank them."

But you can't believe God for something apart from the instruction in His Word. You must obey what His Word says. Only then are you in a position to believe God for the desired results—children who grow up to be obedient, respectful, a lot of fun and who are continually protected from all harm!

This same principle applies not only to discipline, but also to the other prerequisites for divine protection I've

---

1 Chuck Sturgeon, *Train Up Your Child: Inspiration for Today's Christian Parent* (Tulsa: Harrison House Publishers, 1998).

shared with you. First, you must obey what the Word tells you to do: Plead the blood of Jesus over your children, utilize the angelic ministry on their behalf, learn how to listen to your spirit and discipline your children consistently, according to the Word. Then, you can confidently expect what God has promised in His Word—continual, supernatural protection for your family!

Chapter 2

Applying the Blood:
From Passover to Present

As you seek to develop a steadfast confidence in God's protection of your children, nothing is more important than building up your faith in the power resident in the blood of Jesus. The best place I know to start that process is in Exodus. This is where the Lord instituted a vital principle of protection that would forever remain one of His foundational truths: deliverance from death and destruction through sacrificial blood.

Exodus tells us what happened as God worked through Moses to set His people free from their bondage in the land of Egypt. Throughout the entire ordeal, God protected the children of Israel from the plagues devastating the land around them.

In Exodus 12, God instituted the Passover to protect the

Israelites from the final judgment on the people of Egypt—death's visit to every firstborn in the land.

I'm sure the Israelites didn't understand exactly what was going on. Nevertheless, in Exodus 12:3 God instituted a requirement they would have to fulfill to experience this divine protection. God instructed Moses: "In the tenth day of this month they shall take to them every man a lamb, according to the house of their fathers, a lamb for an house." Every Israelite house had to have a lamb.

Thank God, we have a Lamb as well! He's the matchless, precious Lamb of God, Jesus Christ. God appointed Jesus to be the Lamb for our homes.

Keeping an Eternal Memorial by Pleading the Blood

In Exodus 12:14, the Lord went on to say: "And this day shall be unto you for a memorial; and ye shall keep it a feast to the Lord throughout your generations; ye shall keep it a feast by an ordinance for ever."

One thing I've noticed about God is that many times, when He says something is to be kept forever as a memorial in the Old Testament, He gives the Church a way to keep that eternal ordinance in the New Covenant. He doesn't ask us to follow the natural instructions He gave the Israelites, but we can keep His memorial in the spirit.

So let's first see what some of God's original instructions were for the children of Israel to keep the Passover feast. In Exodus 12:7 He says, "And they shall take of the blood, and strike it on the two side posts and on the upper door post of the houses, wherein they shall eat it."

God told His people to apply the blood of the lamb with a hyssop branch to the doorposts of their houses (verse 22) as a memorial to Him forever. The Israelites kept this divine ordinance literally, or in the flesh, but how do we keep it as an eternal memorial in the New Covenant? We keep it in the spiritual realm by pleading the blood of Jesus.

The hyssop branch represents our faith. So, by faith we apply the blood of Jesus to the "doorposts" of our lives with our spoken words. In this way we can daily institute the Passover as an eternal memorial in our lives.

What Does It Mean to "Plead the Blood"?

We need to continually be aware of our spiritual responsibility to plead the blood of Jesus over our children. "But what does it mean to 'plead'?" you may ask. "I don't understand. That sounds like begging."

No, I'm not talking about begging God for anything. The word *plead* is a legal term. It refers to a defendant in a courtroom standing before a judge who asks, "What is your plea—guilty or not guilty?" In the world's court systems, those are the only two choices. But in the high court of heaven, you can declare according to the Word, "I plead the blood!"

The Bible says our enemy, the devil, is the accuser of the brethren. (See Revelation 12:10.) He has his finger in your face, daily, trying to accuse you of something, trying his best to get at you or your family, in order to bring harm and destruction.

But when the accuser stands before the Judge of heaven and says, "This person is guilty," you can say, "No, I am *not* guilty. You can't harm me. This is not mine to take because I'm not standing on my own righteousness. I am standing on the shed blood of Jesus. He paid the price for me. Therefore, I receive His righteousness. I receive His wholeness. I receive His health, His wealth and His well-being!"

That's what you're saying when you say, "I plead the blood." You're saying, "I am innocent by the blood of Jesus. You can't touch me, Devil!"

When you plead the blood as your defense, it doesn't matter if you're guilty or not guilty. The devil has to pass over! (You can always find something to feel guilty about. But, if you *are* guilty, repent.) The devil can't get to you when you plead the blood of Jesus.

In a courtroom, the prosecutor can't do anything to a defendant whom the judge declares innocent. Well, the Judge of all has declared *you* innocent by the blood of Jesus, and the prosecutor—the accuser of the brethren—can't do a thing about it!

One word of caution, though. You can't just know about the power in the blood of Jesus; you must declare it out loud with the words of your mouth. Matthew 12:37 AMP says, "For by your words you will be justified and acquitted, and by your words you will be condemned and sentenced." When you plead the blood of Jesus, you are acquitted instead of condemned. But if you start saying the things the devil wants you to say, you sentence *yourself* to defeat by your own words.

We see, then, that "pleading the blood" is a powerful phrase that lines up with Scripture. It is not just empty religious terminology or an old Pentecostal custom.

Actually, the Pentecostals of old knew some truths about the blood of Jesus the modern Church has let go of. But in the last few years, Christians have begun to regain what the devil had stolen from the Body of Christ about the blood of Jesus.

Personally, I'm believing we won't stop learning until we're walking in the fullness of divine protection and deliverance by the power of the blood.

Putting Our Protection Into Place

Just as the children of Israel applied the blood of a lamb over their doors, we are to plead the blood of Jesus over our lives and the lives of our children. That's the way we put into place the protection God has set aside for us.

For instance, when I enter an airplane, I lay my hand on the door and say, "I plead the blood of Jesus. I apply the blood of Jesus to the doorpost of this airplane. This plane is going to get me where I'm going. My belongings will arrive safely, and the trip will be smooth and without incident." I don't say those words loudly, but I do say them out loud. I don't act strangely or draw attention to myself. But I also don't leave anything out.

My belongings get to my destination better when I plead the blood of Jesus over them. My airplanes arrive where they are supposed to arrive. And as I leave the airplane, I thank the Lord for getting me to my destination safely.

I'm not afraid to get on an airplane, but at the same time, I will not miss the chance to take advantage of what the Lord has given me. I'm going to close and lock every door to the enemy. And I don't care how many people the devil has an assignment against on that airplane—he can't take me down!

I also plead the blood of Jesus every time my family gets in the car to go somewhere. And I make sure my children do the same thing whenever they get behind the wheel.

I want my family protected. In fact, I have made covenant with the Lord and with my family that we are not going to be taken out of this world through tragedy, accidents or any other strategy of the devil. We are not going to let the enemy have control over us.

We are going to go together in the Rapture. Or if the Lord tarries, we will all live to an old age. We won't go home to heaven until we are satisfied that we have completed what God has called us to do on this earth.

That's what you need to do with your family. Settle it in your heart before heaven and earth that the devil isn't going to take out any member of your family through his strategies. Don't wait until your child is in a coma or until you're standing in a bank during a robbery. Make that covenant with the Lord right now.

That decision will give you the determination to hold fast to the Word when a storm comes. It will also keep you from listening to the devil when he tries to convince you, "This tragedy is God's will for you."

No, it isn't God's will! God's will is not that you or your children suffer harm or perish, but that you live a long life. He needs us all to help fulfill His purposes on this earth.

It seems so absurd when you think about it. Why would God try to kill you and your family members if He needs every one of you? A landowner doesn't send all the field hands back to the main house for a rest at peak harvest time!

God's Way to Escape Judgment

When you continually apply the blood of Jesus to the doorposts of your life by faith, you can live in complete confidence that the devil can't touch your family because God has them in His hands.

But why is this so? Why can't the devil gain access to your family when you plead the blood of Jesus over them every day? To answer that question, we have to understand the way God provided for us to escape judgment. Let's go back to Exodus 12:12:

> For I will pass through the land of Egypt this night, and will smite all the firstborn in the land of Egypt, both man and beast; and against all the gods of Egypt I will execute judgment: I am the Lord.

When death passed through Egypt, the only reason it was able to kill every firstborn was that the Egyptians lacked any divine protection. When God said, "I will execute judgment," He didn't mean He was going to *send* death just to see how many people He could kill. He simply meant death would pass through the land, and because the Egyptians were not protected behind the blood, they would be subject to judgment.

But in the land of Goshen, God had given the Israelites a

way out. In verse 13, He said, "And the blood shall be to you for a token upon the houses where ye are: and when I see the blood, I will pass over you." The Israelites had the choice to either accept or reject God's way. Those who obeyed God's command to apply the blood of a lamb to their doors were protected behind the blood and escaped judgment when death passed through.

Well, nothing has changed since then. When the blood is present, death still can't come in. However, today we no longer apply the blood of a literal lamb to our doorposts. Now we have the blood of Jesus to protect us. He shed His blood once and for all to purchase our complete deliverance from every work of the enemy.

Notice God said, "The blood shall be to you for a token upon the houses where ye are." The blood of the lamb was a token, or a showing, of God's power. Death saw that token and couldn't prevail against it.

Today we don't have just a token, we have the real thing. How much more does the devil see the blood of Jesus covering our families and knows he cannot prevail against us?

Poor Children in a Rich Father's House

Sadly, many Christians choose to live their lives without applying the blood of Jesus to the doorposts of their lives. Failing to actively believe God for protection, they leave themselves vulnerable to the devil's attacks.

But we can't afford to be passive about protection. We're living in a horrible day. In the words of Charles Dickens, it is both the best of times and the worst of times.

For those in the world, it is a dangerous time, without hope. Disasters and tragedies abound, and the chances are good that, at some point in their lives, most people will be caught in one of them. They may become victims of crime, car accidents or earthquakes that kill thousands. Regardless of the circumstances in which these people find themselves, one thing is sure—without the blood of Jesus, they have no supernatural recourse nor hope of deliverance.

Christians are not in that plight. They do have a way of escape but are often ignorant of it. They don't know they can live each day with a shield of divine protection around them. Nor do they know they don't have to be pushed to and fro with the world, according to the devil's whims. Therefore, they live their entire lives receiving only one benefit of Jesus' blood—the right to go to heaven when they die. They never know what it is to live a separated life, protected from all harm by the blood of Jesus.

What a shame that is! It's like being a member of a rich family, yet living in poverty all your life, without anything good to eat, decent clothes to wear or a decent home to live in. But you do know that when you die, they'll build a beautiful golden crypt to lay your body in!

That's the way God sees it when His people don't appropriate the divine protection He has provided. It's just like any other promise in the Word of God. If Christians don't believe God for protection, they aren't going to enjoy the benefits of that particular promise. The blessing of supernatural protection will go unclaimed and unused unless they learn how to receive it from their heavenly Father.

Strangers From the Covenant

Some Christians even pray, "If I die before I wake, I pray the Lord my soul to take." Not only are these people unsure whether or not they will die before they wake up, but they aren't even sure the Lord will take their soul if they do!

Doubting God's ability to protect His children is an example of religious thinking, which the enemy uses to keep Christians defeated and under his thumb.

Because of religious traditions, people have not received the blood of Jesus as a true and practical help in their every-day lives. "For [although] they hold a form of piety (true religion), they deny and reject and are strangers to the power of it..." (2 Timothy 3:5 AMP).

According to Ephesians 2:12-13, 19, we have been brought near to God and His promises by the blood:

> That at that time ye were without Christ, being
> aliens from the commonwealth of Israel, and
> strangers from the covenants of promise, having
> no hope, and without God in the world: But
> now in Christ Jesus ye who sometimes were far
> off are made nigh by the blood of Christ.... Now
> therefore ye are no more strangers and foreign-
> ers, but fellow citizens with the saints, and of the
> household of God.

We are no longer strangers to the covenants of promise.
What a shame to live as though we were! Without realizing
it, we have often doubted the power of and thereby spurned
the blood of Jesus by not putting it into action in our lives or
in the lives of our children. When we have been afraid of
something the enemy is trying to do to our families, for
instance, we have discounted the blood of Jesus as our
answer. In essence, we have been saying, "Well, the blood
can't do the job here. This is just too big for God." We have
denied the power of the blood of Jesus and settled for religion. In so doing, we have dishonored His blood.

When people receive salvation but don't experience any
life change, healing or prosperity as a result of it, they are
essentially spurning the blood and many other precious
promises because religion—traditions of men—has caused

them to be strangers from the covenants of promise. The same is true of church denominations which have taken songs about the blood out of their hymnals, claiming such songs "scare" the children.

The blood of Jesus is the very key to our existence. It is our very life. We, as believers, must honor the blood above sin, sickness, problems or lack. After all, isn't that exactly what the Father did? He honored Jesus' blood over our sin. He declared us free from sickness because of the blood shed on our behalf. We must lay hold of it and receive it as more than just a church tradition or a Bible story.

The Church cannot survive in power without a real revelation of the blood of Jesus. The devil knows this, so one of his main tricks is to keep Christians from knowing about the sure protection available to them through the blood. Even many Word-believing, Spirit-filled Christians haven't been able to firmly lay hold of their deliverance because they haven't understood the power in the blood of Jesus. Therefore, they doubt God's ability to protect them and their families from all harm.

Praise God, doubt is erased as we begin to receive the benefits purchased for us through the precious blood of Jesus. We will never again be as strangers and outsiders, living as though we had no covenant with God. How that grieves the Holy Spirit!

The Holy Spirit is the Minister of grace. It is His delight to deliver us through the saving power of the blood. Therefore, it grieves Him when He is restrained, by our disobedience, from imparting the grace to protect, heal and prosper us. He isn't grieved for Jesus' sake, but for our sakes. He is limited in ministering His blessings to us unless we honor, highly prize and appropriate the blood of Jesus in our lives.

Understanding the Nature of Judgment

We saw in Exodus 12:12 that God said He would execute judgment. To understand what He meant by this, we must first understand the true nature of judgment.

First, it's important to understand that God didn't invent sin. Everything He created was good. It was the devil who introduced sin, and he has been twisting God's perfect creation ever since.

Second, judgment is not God beating people over the head because they have sinned. God doesn't say, "Well, he did this wrong, so I'm going to give him cancer or AIDS to teach him a lesson."

God already decreed that the wages of sin is death (Romans 6:23). He was saying that death is what sin leads to, and death will be the price that must be paid.

That one verse alone, tells us what we need to know about the nature of judgment. It tells us that if we practice sin, we open the door to the enemy's works of death and destruction.

After God decreed that the wages of sin is death, there was no getting around that judgment because He spoke the truth. He laid out that eternal principle for us once, and He never has to do it again. Psalm 111:7-8 AMP confirms this:

> The works of His hands are [absolute] truth and justice [faithful and right]; and all His decrees and precepts are sure (fixed, established, and trustworthy). They stand fast and are established forever and ever and are done in [absolute] truth and uprightness.

All God's decrees are fixed. That's the way it is. Those divine decrees aren't going to change, and anything that goes against them will reap the reward of judgment.

God doesn't have to judge every situation. He isn't out there saying, "I'm going to do this to judge that sin, and I'll do that to judge this other sin." His decree against sin stands. He doesn't see a sinner today and say, "You're living a homosexual lifestyle, so I am going to strike you with AIDS." He has already decreed that sin leads to death. That's the way it is, and it is not going to change.

Think for a moment about the way lawyers argue their case before a judge in a court of law. Lawyers often refer to a list of cases that support the way they want the judgment to go. They do that to demonstrate that in similar cases, other judges have already made a decision. The lawyers hope that the current judge will agree with those past decisions and rule in their favor.

A well-known example of a settled judgment is in the case of Roe v. Wade, the landmark Supreme Court case of 1973 that opened the door for legalized abortion in the United States. Without a move of God that Supreme Court judgment supporting abortion will stand up in court. There is no need for a lawyer in a lower court to argue the issue again. Why? Because the judgment has already been made. Until a new law is passed, abortion will be legal—even if it is not moral.

That's also the way judgment works as far as God is concerned. He has already determined that the wages of sin is death. Therefore, as sin runs rampant on the earth, judgment occurs because of that previously established spiritual law.

That's why God told the children of Israel, "If you will do what I tell you to do, you will be blessed. If you don't, the curse will come on you." (See Deuteronomy 28.)

God didn't create those curses. Nor did He create the repercussions of sin. Sin caused the curse. God just tells us how to avoid its results. He lets us know that sin is a path that inevitably leads to death and destruction.

So when you think about all the bad things that happen

in this earth, realize those calamities are just the natural destination to which sin leads. There's no way to get away from it apart from the saving power of Jesus. You have to get on a different road and start heading a different direction in order to arrive at a different destination.

My father, Kenneth Copeland, gave a wonderful illustration of this that I can't improve on. Suppose you are driving down a highway and read a sign that says, "Austin, 200 miles." If you don't want to go to Austin, you'd better make a U-turn—because if you stay on that road, you'll end up in Austin!

In the same way, God puts up signposts to let you know which way you're headed spiritually. If you stay on the road to sin, or don't actively do something to get off that road, you're going to end up in judgment. So if you don't want to end up there, you had better turn around.

Having decreed that the wages of sin is death, God graciously gave everyone who has ever lived on this earth a way to escape judgment through the death and resurrection of His Son, Jesus Christ. Even before Jesus came, God provided a temporary way of escape through the sacrificial blood of animals. He has never failed to provide man with a way of escape.

So how do you get off the road to judgment? And how do you make sure your children stay off that road so they can reach God's destination of deliverance and victory? By obeying the fixed decree that God instituted on the night of the Passover: When the blood is present, death cannot come in. You apply the blood of Jesus to the doorposts of your life with your words, and you never stop speaking the protection of the blood for you and your family, by faith!

God Isn't the Source of Calamity

A lot of Christians tell people that tragedy is God judging their sins. But that isn't true. Tragedy and trouble are not from God. Good is from God, and bad is from the devil. It's just that simple. Actually, it's too simple to mess up, but we seem to find a way to do it anyway!

God has been so maligned in these last days. His Name has been so dishonored with false accusations. People say all the time, "God caused that disaster" or "God allowed that tragedy to happen." These people think God is behind the horrible things they hear on the news, whether it is school shootings, fatal accidents or natural disasters.

But God is not the One causing those tragic events. The terrible things that happen in the world are not "acts of God," nor are they God's way of punishing people or bringing them to a low point where they will finally repent. That's not what judgment is.

Actually, people who think God causes bad things to happen by His sovereign will are not thinking that premise all the way through. Otherwise, they would see that it just doesn't make sense.

Tragedy is not God's will. We know that because we have a copy of His will—the written Word of God—the Bible. It says, "Every *good* gift and every perfect gift is from above, and cometh down from the Father of lights, with whom is no variableness, neither shadow of turning" (James 1:17). Our heavenly Father gives only good and perfect gifts. Tragedy is part of the devil's bag of tricks—part of the judgment to which sin inevitably leads.

Actually, the simplest way to define judgment is this: As the earth fills up with sin, the overflow is judgment.

The world has been on a fast track to judgment for a number of years now. Just watch the evening news, and you'll see what I mean! When you can watch a doctor kill someone on a television news documentary and it is deemed acceptable, or when millions of unborn babies can be killed and it doesn't bother too many people—you know the earth is filling up with sin!

This earth is groaning and shaking under the burden of mankind's sin. And when that sin overflows, the end result is an increase in judgment.

Just as judgment went through the land of Egypt on the night of the Passover , today, judgment is sweeping through the earth in an unprecedented measure. We are witnessing more calamities and large-scale natural disasters around the world than ever before. As an example, just consider the January 25, 2001, earthquake in India that killed more than 20,000 people!

Governments might try to make things better through programs and policies. However, ultimately, there is nothing *man* can do to stem the tide of judgment on the earth.

But God has already done something! He sent His Son, Jesus, to give all people a way out. He is doing everything He possibly can to change people's hearts and help them start living for Him so they can get off the road to judgment.

The truth is, although the earth is filling up with sin in this hour, it is also filling up with God's glory. Romans 5:20 says that where sin abounds, grace does much more abound!

That divine grace will protect you and your children, even if you find yourselves in a place where judgment is occurring. You may ask, "But how could God deliver us in the middle of an earthquake that kills 30,000 people?" Well, Psalm 91:7 says, "A thousand shall fall at thy side, and ten thousand at thy right hand; but it shall not come nigh thee." God says He can and will protect you, even when death and destruction are all around you. The promise is there if you want to claim it and are willing to apply the blood of Jesus to the doorposts of your life.

The Case of God's Sovereignty

The lie that God is behind both the man-made and the natural disasters that happen in this world is just a trick of the devil to keep us from trusting God and appropriating His promise of protection in our lives. If we believed that lie we would conclude that "God is sovereign, so I have no control over what might happen to my family and me in the future. Since God is sovereign, whatever happens to me is His will. I just have to bear it because it's all part of His plan." But that's a very deadly thought process that will keep believers from being able to move into what God wants them to do. Suppose, for example, these Christians were in a situation where a terrorist was pointing a gun at them and they sensed the Holy Spirit prompting them to walk over to the criminal and boldly share the gospel with him. Without a solid assurance of God's protection, how would they be able to do that?

If you believe whatever happens, good or bad, is God's will, how can you have any confidence God will protect you or your children from all harm? Yes, God is sovereign. But He sovereignly gave us dominion over the enemy through the Name of Jesus, the blood of Jesus and the anointed Word. (See Luke 10:19; Mark 16:15-20; Matthew 10:7-8; Revelation 12:11, to list a few!) He sovereignly gave us covenant promises and sovereignly decided to give us the choice whether or not to appropriate those promises.

God will not take back that choice. He isn't going to change. Everything would cease to exist if He were to turn back on His Word and do something different than what He has already said—because what He has said is truth.

When tragedy hits, many Christians who argue the

sovereignty of God say, "Well, it must have been God's will, or this terrible tragedy wouldn't have happened to me."

That is such a spiritually lazy way to look at life! People with this viewpoint are actually saying, "I have no part to play in what happens to me."

No, that's wrong! God's Word says we are to be alert and vigilant against the devil's attacks (1 Peter 5:8-9). We can't just go around thinking, *I'm a Christian, so God is going to protect me*, and then assume He will prevent anything bad from happening to us.

Protection is not automatic. In fact, I haven't found anything in God's Word that is automatic. Even salvation must be believed, asked for and received.

For some reason, we seem to think God's promises are going to be fulfilled for us just because we're Christians. But it just doesn't work that way. Someone once said to me, "But I thought when you got saved you were automatically protected."

The Spirit of God spoke up inside me and I told her, "Well, that would be true if the enemy weren't trying every day to...," and finishing my sentence, she added, "...take it away from you!" I saw the light come on in her eyes.

God has placed the responsibility in our laps to find out what He has to say and then appropriate it into our lives.

If we don't fulfill our God-ordained responsibility, we'll go along with the world's flow until we end up caught in judgment somewhere, just like everyone else. Sure, we'll get to heaven (possibly sooner than planned!), but we could have gotten there a lot more easily and a lot more protected.

I'll give you an example of another dangerous way Christians often think. A couple who has just suffered the loss of their baby might go to a pastor for counsel and hear these "comforting" words: "Well, God must have needed a flower for His garden. He needed your little baby to come home to Him."

What an insult to God! What a trampling of the blood of Jesus to say that something the enemy has done is the work of God!

Be very careful not to say such words yourself. It will hinder your ability to receive the promises of God in your own life. It's better to say, "I don't know how I let this happen, but I'm going to search the Word and see what God says about it."

God will answer your questions, but not when you come to Him accusingly and ask, "Lord, why did You do this?" Anger toward God is always self-defeating. The devil will use it to take you further from the answer and further from God.

God once said something arresting to me on my way to teach high-school students about the divine protection afforded us by the blood of Jesus. I'll never forget the pain in His voice as He said, *I have a hard time convincing My children to trust Me fully with their lives because they still don't firmly believe I'll deliver and protect them.*

I understood what the Lord was trying to get across to me. After all, it's very difficult to have courage in what you do for the Lord if you're not assured of His protection. If you think He allows tragedies to occur in your life to teach you something, you'll find it difficult to entrust your life, or your children's lives, to Him.

God was saying, "My people won't give their lives fully to Me because they don't trust Me. How can they trust Me if they think I might decide that allowing their child to be martyred is the best way to further the gospel?"

God knows what it's like to be a parent. He is a Father! He knows what it is to see a Son die. But, praise His Name—because He knew that pain, we don't have to! He is offering us assurance that our children will be protected and He says we can have that strong assurance! All we have to do is walk in the light of His Word and appropriate His promise of protection.

Just imagine Jesus walking on this earth today. If someone held a gun to His face, would He be afraid He might get shot? Absolutely not! Jesus would know beyond a shadow of a doubt His Father would deliver Him.

Well, God will deliver our children, too. We just need to get off the road to judgment the world is on and start going the other way—protecting our children with the precious blood of Jesus!

CHAPTER 3

Protection Through God's Grace

O ne of the most important things I've learned about the blood of Jesus is this: When we plead the blood of Jesus over our children, we make allowances for their mistakes, as well as our own mistakes and shortcomings. (Now, don't get religious on me!) Let me explain.

That doesn't mean we can live any way we want to live. But it does mean God has made a way out of the place of judgment for us. Through the blood of Jesus, He has set us free from the guilt of sin. First John 1:7 says it very plainly: "But if we walk in the light, as he is in the light, we have fellowship one with another, and the blood of Jesus Christ his Son cleanseth us from all sin."

No Weapon Shall Prosper Because of the Blood

Look at Isaiah 54:17, one of my favorite scriptures. It's part of a very powerful chapter full of promises you can stake your life on.

The Lord recently opened up this verse to me to help me understand how divine protection is available by the blood of Jesus through the avenue of His grace.

> No weapon that is formed against thee shall prosper; and every tongue that shall rise against thee in judgment thou shalt condemn. This is the heritage of the servants of the Lord, and their righteousness is of me, saith the Lord.

The Lord brought this scripture to my mind sometime ago when we arrived at the scene of an accident on the way to take the kids to Superkid Academy Camp. A mother had made the mistake of having more children in her van than she had seatbelts. She also let her 16-year-old son drive the overloaded van on country roads. As her son drove around a corner a little too fast, the van went off the road and rolled several times, totaling the vehicle.

I was not far behind them with my own children and two other junior counselors. Shortly after the van went off the road, we came to the detour that had been set up because of the accident. I thought, *I'd better turn around and see if that accident involved any of our campers.*

Sure enough, it did. The emergency personnel were already there, checking all the occupants of the van for injuries. I drove up and spoke to one of the emergency workers on the scene. He told me, "I can't believe no one was hurt in this accident. They should have all been hurt!"

What was the devil trying to do? He was trying to ruin Superkid Academy Camp for the summer, ruin the lives of the four families represented in the van and take out some powerful, on-fire Christian kids who know how to pray and believe the Word. And, he was trying to ruin the lives of that mother and her son. Just think what it would have been like for them had any lives been lost while that young man was driving!

The devil had attempted to steal, kill and destroy everything he could in this situation and to take out anyone he could. But he wasn't able to do it.

The van was lying in a big field next to the road and looked just awful. But not one of the children had been hurt in the accident. Even the ones not wearing seatbelts had escaped without a scratch! The only person injured at all was the mother, who sustained a few cuts on her arm.

We piled everyone into the cars of others headed to the camp who had stopped to help. The young man who had been driving the van rode with me. On our way to the campgrounds, the Lord put it on my heart to minister to this young man because he was feeling very guilty.

I said, "Let me ask you something. Did you plead the blood of Jesus this morning?"

"Well, yes," he replied. "We plead the blood of Jesus whenever we go anywhere. This morning we also prayed and took Communion before we left."

The young man continued, "I knew I shouldn't have been driving. I had thoughts that something might happen."

I said, "Well, it is important to listen to your spirit."

Right then the Lord reminded me of Isaiah 54:17, and I realized why He had supernaturally protected everyone involved in the accident, though mistakes were made.

This verse says, "No weapon that is formed against thee shall prosper." It also says "every tongue that shall rise against thee in judgment thou shalt condemn." In this case, it was the devil's wagging tongue that rose up in judgment against the mother and son saying, "You messed up, so I'm going to kill someone today. I'm going to ruin someone's life today."

The devil isn't just trying to be an inconvenience in his strategies against you or your children. His goal is to kill and destroy. In every way he can, he's trying to get rid of you.

But the devil can't do that if you don't allow him to! God promises in this verse that no weapon formed against you will succeed in its evil intent. Then He says, "This is the heritage of the servants of the Lord, and their righteousness is of me, saith the Lord."

Walking in Jesus' Footsteps

The Lord was giving me all these insights so I could share them with this young man as we were driving along to camp. Then I said something I had never thought of before.

I told the teenager, "You weren't walking in your own righteousness today, so don't let the devil lie to you and convince you that you're guilty. You pled the blood of Jesus. And even though you messed up—even though you shouldn't have driven with more kids in the car than you had seatbelts—this is what the Lord told me: *When you plead the blood of Jesus, you put yourself in His footsteps. You are purposely living your life in His righteousness, and the devil can't fight that.*

"Now, as a child," I continued, "it is important that you obey your parents. And when God prompts you to do something, it is important to listen to your spirit. It is also important to obey the laws of the land. But when we plead the blood of Jesus, we make allowances for our own mistakes and shortcomings—for the times we don't pick up on what the Holy Spirit is saying to us."

It's always easier to do something the right way. There's almost certainly going to be an irritating price to pay when you're disobedient or when you don't listen to the Spirit of God.

For instance, that mother's van was totaled. She also had to go to a doctor so the cuts on her arm could be stitched up. Those consequences for her mistake were definitely annoying, but not life threatening.

That's the effect of divine protection. When you plead the blood of Jesus by faith, God will deliver you to the other side without loss of life—whether yours, your children's or your spouse's. You may endure inconvenient consequences for not listening to God, but you'll not suffer irreversible tragedy.

On the other hand, you can't just go along sinning on purpose, living your life any old way you want to, and then say, "Well, I'll just plead the blood, and everything will be OK."

In the case of the van accident, that mother and son didn't set out on that trip trying to see how much they could get away with, with God. They weren't trying to blatantly go against the Lord's instructions. Their hearts were right—they just missed it.

Psalm 24:3-4 says we have to come to God with clean hands and pure hearts. We can't live a sinful life and then expect everything to go right for us.

Although it's true that we have to maintain a pure heart, it is also true we all mess up sometimes. In light of this fact, isn't it good to know God doesn't require 100-percent perfection at this stage of the game? Instead, He has made it possible for us to walk in the footsteps of Jesus, in *His* 100-percent perfection, clothed in His righteousness and not our own.

We are headed toward a goal, learning to listen to our spirits and to hear the voice of the Holy Spirit. We are endeavoring to do the right thing in every situation, and we purpose to plead the blood of Jesus over our families every day. As we do these things, the devil won't be able to touch our children or us.

But, if we mess up during this learning process, we can be confident, as long as we keep our families under the protection of the blood: Our mistakes may cost us some time and money, but not our lives or the lives of our children. If we will faithfully plead the blood of Jesus, God will deliver us and our families—with our lives intact. That's a promise we can claim!

So, if you do something wrong or miss the Spirit of God's leading, just repent and say, "I plead not guilty, because I plead the blood of Jesus!" Your faith in the blood puts you in Jesus' footsteps and provides you and your children with divine protection—all because of God's grace.

What Is Grace?

I've heard many definitions for *grace*. One definition says *grace* is "unmerited favor," another, that it is "God's ability to do things you can't do." But the best definition I've ever heard is: "Grace is God looking at you the same way He looks at His Son. It is God judging you as though you were Jesus."

What does that mean for you? Well, can you imagine the heavenly Father looking at Jesus and saying, "I'm not going to do that for You"? Absolutely not!

Jesus died in your place and shed His blood so you could stand in His righteousness. As you plead the blood of Jesus over your family, God sees you and your loved ones the same way He sees Jesus—deserving of the same blessings and the same angelic protection He afforded His Son when He walked this earth.

How does God see Jesus? Well, He sees a Son who doesn't make mistakes. He judges Jesus to be free from sickness, sin, calamity and spiritual death. The good news is that Jesus paid the price for you so you could be free as well!

When you appropriate the blood of Jesus in your life, God looks at you and says, "You're free, you're clean and you're in My righteousness. You are covered by My wings."

The devil would love to lie to you and say, "God can't deliver you from this mess because you brought it on yourself."

But as you and your family stand in Jesus' footsteps, it doesn't matter if you've made mistakes or if your children mess up. It doesn't matter if you're guilty or innocent because God's deliverance isn't based on you—it's based on Jesus. As you plead the blood of Jesus, His grace covers your mistakes, as you live in His righteousness.

For example, you may ask, "Yes, but what if my mistake

involves a lot of charge card debt?"

The devil has kept so many believers bowed down with guilt and discouragement because of this particular problem. The enemy whispers to their minds, "God can't deliver you from charge card debt because you used your card to charge an entire closet full of clothes with it! That was selfish. You knew better than to do that. God can't deliver you because you put *yourself* in that situation."

But God judges us according to the way He sees Jesus, and Jesus doesn't have charge card problems. That means we are judged free from charge card problems, too.

We can come before God and say, "Lord, I repent. Please deliver me from debt. I plead the blood of Jesus over my finances." God then judges us with the same favor He gives Jesus and responds, *You are perfect in My eyes. Therefore, I gladly deliver you from debt!* That is a manifestation of His grace!

Here's another example: The devil accuses a person in his mind, saying, "God can't heal you from cancer because you smoked. You knew it was bad for you, but you did it anyway for years and years and years."

But Jesus doesn't have a problem with smoking. God doesn't look at Jesus and say, "Well, I can't heal You of lung cancer because You used to smoke."

So God looks at that believer and makes a judgment

based on how He judges Jesus. Even if that person smoked for most of his life, he can still trust in God's measureless grace and therefore stand confidently on God's promise to heal his body.

In the same way, God protects us as though we were Jesus when we walk in His righteousness. And the Word says that Jesus could have called 10,000 angels to help Him. (See Matthew 26:53.) If He could, we can!

The Source of God's Grace

Why is this true? Romans 5:21 gives us the answer. It says that grace reigns through righteousness. Jesus' righteousness is the doorway through which God's grace enters our lives.

God can provide grace for us because we are made righteous through the blood of Jesus. He now sees us the way He sees Jesus. His grace on our lives isn't based on our good works or our perfection but on *His* perfection. As Isaiah 54:17 says, "Their righteousness is of me, saith the Lord."

That's why no weapon formed against you or your children can prosper. When you plead the blood of Jesus over your family, you are living fully in the righteousness of Jesus. You and your children are literally standing before the Father in the footsteps of Jesus. You can therefore say, "It doesn't matter what I or my children did wrong. It doesn't matter if we are guilty or not guilty. I plead the blood! I receive the righteousness of Jesus."

Too many Christians are trying to base their protection on their own ability. They have forgotten their covenant of divine protection. They might say a little prayer and read a scripture or two in the morning. But then they go on, trying to get through the day on their own.

But when you plead the blood of Jesus over yourself and your children each morning, it does something to you. It sets your mind and spirit right to realize at the beginning of each day, *My family is getting through this day protected by the grace of God and the blood of Jesus.*

Draw Near for Righteous Judgments

Isaiah 58:2 AMP talks about the children of Israel coming to God for righteous judgments.

> Yet they [God's people] seek, inquire for, and require Me daily and delight [externally] to know My ways, as [if they were in reality] a nation that did righteousness and forsook not the ordinance of their God. They ask of Me righteous judgments, they delight to draw near to God [in visible ways].

When read in context, we can see God is actually correcting

His people, telling them that their spiritual actions need to be a reflection of an inward change of heart. But lets look at how He describes those actions: "They ask of Me righteous judgments, they delight to draw near to God."

That's similar to the New Covenant admonition to draw near to the throne of grace (Hebrews 4:16 AMP). You have already been given a righteous judgment. God has made you the righteousness of God in Christ (2 Corinthians 5:21). He has given you promises already bought and paid for by the blood of His Son. Those promises belong to you and your family. Now, you just have to lay hold of them, standing on His righteous judgments by faith in the blood of Jesus.

As you plead the blood of Jesus, you are coming boldly before God's throne, according to His righteous judgment, to receive His mercy and grace for your family. You're saying, "We're not perfect in ourselves, Lord, but I plead the blood of Jesus over our lives so we can walk in Your footsteps. I want my family to live in Your righteousness today." When you do that, God is always faithful to give you His grace!

When you enter His throne room based on the blood of Jesus, you are coming to the Father, asking Him to judge you with the same "measuring stick" with which He judges Jesus. And when He does what you ask, the miracle of grace is that you actually do measure up!

You don't have to live according to the way of the world. You don't have to live subject to the tricks of the enemy or to the misguided people who follow him. You and your children can live every day in the footsteps of Jesus!

For instance, suppose Jesus, in His glorified body, lived on this earth today, and was standing in a bank, when thieves burst in to rob it. There's no way those thieves would be able to hurt Him. He would be able to turn that entire situation around!

Well, that's who you are. You have Jesus Christ on the inside of you. And when you plead His blood, you make yourself more aware of who you are in Him.

As you faithfully plead the blood of Jesus over yourself and your children daily, not only does it change the circumstances that surround you, but it changes you. It changes the way you react in difficult situations.

It is easier to respond with confidence and faith when you know you're standing in Jesus' footsteps. No matter what the circumstances, you can rest in the knowledge that your family is protected from harm by the precious blood of Jesus—because grace reigns through righteousness, and you are righteous in Christ!

Our Sanctuary—
The Holy of Holies

I want to take you to some key scriptures to show you two basic principles for protecting your children. First, your deliverance from evil, tragedy, sickness or sudden death is by faith in the blood of Jesus. Second, your faith in the blood is entered into and executed by the words of your mouth.

I also want to show you why these two principles are true. It all has to do with entering the holy of holies—the eternal sanctuary of God's presence.

The Way Into God's Presence—By Blood

Let's start by going back to the Old Testament and seeing

how God made a way for His people to enter His presence by means of sacrificial blood:

> The Lord said to Moses, Tell Aaron your brother he must not come at all times into the Holy of Holies within the veil before the mercy seat upon the ark, lest he die; for I will appear in the cloud on the mercy seat (Leviticus 16:2 AMP).

Moses' brother, Aaron, was the high priest, but he couldn't just go into the holy of holies anytime or any way he wanted to. He could only go in once a year at the appointed time, and had to do everything just as God had instructed.

The high priest couldn't forget the smallest detail. He had to wash the right way, say the right things and sprinkle the blood of the right kind of animals. He had to follow God's instructions to the letter. If the high priest's sin wasn't covered when he went in to the presence of God, he wouldn't come out alive!

That didn't mean God was trying to make it hard for His people to come to Him. He wasn't trying to separate Himself from man because He was prideful. God was actually protecting man. He knew sin could not exist in His presence.

Darkness cannot live in the light. The smallest bit of light can dispel darkness, but darkness cannot overcome light.

That's why God couldn't gather Adam and Eve in His arms to comfort them after they had sinned. That would be the natural instinct of any loving father. But if God had done that, His goodness would have killed them because sin is destroyed in the presence of His glory.

So God, in His mercy, made a way for fallen man to draw near to Him. He instituted the slaying of an animal whose innocent blood acted as a temporary remedy for sin. In Leviticus 16, He gave detailed instructions to the high priest, the people's representative, on how to enter into His presence. It had to be by blood, and done just the right way. (Read the rest of Leviticus 16, and you'll see what I mean!)

The high priest's job was to take the blood of that sacrifice and enter God's presence for the sole purpose of obtaining a good judgment for himself and for the people. If the priest did everything correctly, he and the people would be judged free from sin for one year.

Draw Near by the Blood

Interestingly, the Hebrew word for *sacrifice* is from the same root as "to come near, to approach, to become closely involved in a relationship with someone."[2] The blood of the sacrificial animal enabled the high priest to enter the holy of

---

2   *The Holy Temple of Jerusalem*, Chaim Richman, The Temple Institute and Carta, Jerusalem, 1977 Carta, The Israel Map and Publishing Company, Ltd.

holies and draw near to the mercy seat of God. Had the high priest not brought the blood of that sacrifice, the sin in his own life would have killed him before he ever reached the mercy seat.

It wasn't that God needed a gift from the people or wanted them to do something for Him. Man needed the blood to atone for his sin so he could draw near to God.

Well, today we have the blood of Jesus, who was the perfect Sacrifice. His precious blood takes care of our sin once and for all, allowing us to draw near to the throne of God to receive mercy and grace for every situation.

Hebrews 9:12-14 AMP tells us the magnitude of what Jesus did for us through His death and resurrection:

> He went once for all into the [Holy of] Holies [of heaven], not by virtue of the blood of goats and calves [by which to make reconciliation between God and man], but His own blood, having found and secured a complete redemption (an everlasting release for us). For if [the mere] sprinkling of unholy and defiled persons with blood of goats and bulls and with the ashes of a burnt heifer is sufficient for the purification of the body, how much more surely shall the blood of Christ, Who by virtue of [His] eternal Spirit [His own preexistent divine personality] has offered Himself as an

unblemished sacrifice to God, purify our con-
sciences from dead works and lifeless observances
to serve the [ever] living God?

God is saying here, "If a goat, a bull or a heifer could
provide a temporary redemption for sin under the old covenant, how much more will the blood of Jesus Christ provide
an eternal and absolutely complete redemption for you
under the new covenant?"

Let's go on to verses 18-20 AMP:

So even the [old] first covenant (God's will) was
not inaugurated and ratified and put in force
without the shedding of blood. For when every
command of the Law had been read out by
Moses to all the people, he took the blood of
slain calves and goats, together with water and
scarlet wool and a bunch of hyssop, and sprinkled both the Book (the roll of the Law and
covenant) itself and all the people, saying these
words: This is the blood that seals and ratifies
the agreement (the testament, the covenant)
which God commanded [me to deliver to] you.

Under the old covenant, Moses used a bunch of hyssop

(which symbolizes our faith) to sprinkle the blood of the animal sacrifice over the people as atonement for their sins. Then he declared, "This is the blood that seals and ratifies our covenant with God!"

Notice that Moses spoke those words out loud. This was an Old Testament demonstration of the important principle I mentioned earlier, that our faith in the blood is executed and entered into by the words of our mouths.

Instead of hyssop, we use faith to apply the blood of Jesus to our lives. But as we plead the blood of Jesus over ourselves and our children by faith, we are actually saying the same thing Moses said: "This is the blood that seals and ratifies the covenant I have with You, Lord. And part of that covenant is Your promise to protect us!"

Verse 22 tells us why our approach to God must be by means of sacrificial blood:

> [In fact] under the Law almost everything is purified by means of blood, and without the shedding of blood there is neither release from sin and its guilt nor the remission of the due and merited punishment for sins.

Aaron went into the holy of holies with the blood of an animal. But Jesus took His very own blood into God's presence. In doing so, He made the way, tearing down the veil that had always separated man from the presence of God.

Jesus, the "Lamb for our house," paid the price to enter into the holy of holies by the power of His blood. The only thing left for us to do is apply the blood He shed for us to our lives—to declare by faith, "This is the blood that seals my covenant with God!"

As we do this, we are purified and set free not only from sin, but also from all things pertaining to death and judgment—the due and merited punishment for our sin. We can now enter the holy of holies by the power in the blood of Jesus, according to Hebrews 10:19-20 AMP:

> Therefore, brethren, since we have full freedom and confidence to enter into the [Holy of] Holies [by the power and virtue] in the blood of Jesus, by this fresh (new) and living way which He initiated and dedicated and opened for us through the separating curtain (veil of the Holy of Holies), that is, through His flesh.

Jesus entered the place where no sin could go. He had already carried all our sin to the Cross and to hell, paying the price with His own blood. But then He arose and ascended to the heavenly holy of holies, where He sprinkled His own blood on the mercy seat of God once and for all, for us.

If most people were God, I believe they would have stopped right there. They would have let Jesus be the only One who could enter the holy of holies. But God never stops halfway. In verses 21-22 AMP, He invites *us* to enter the holy of holies:

> And since we have [such] a great and wonderful and noble Priest [Who rules] over the house of God, let us all come forward and draw near with true (honest and sincere) hearts in unqualified assurance and absolute conviction engendered by faith (by that leaning of the entire human personality on God in absolute trust and confidence in His power, wisdom, and goodness), having our hearts sprinkled and purified from a guilty (evil) conscience and our bodies cleansed with pure water.

God invites you to come into His throne room where no sin can come. How can you do that if you're not perfect? Only by the blood of Jesus! By pleading the blood of Jesus, you may confidently approach the throne of God with clean hands and a pure heart. This has a greater meaning than we have realized.

The Devil Can't Cross the Blood Line

When I first began to gain an understanding about the blood of Jesus, I would hear Billye Brim say, "When you plead the blood of Jesus, you draw a circle around your home and your family, and the devil can't cross that blood line."

Well, that made sense to me. I knew it was true and I believed it. But I wanted to know why. Why is it that when you plead the blood of Jesus, the devil can't cross that line? So I began searching the Word, and the Lord gave me some answers to my questions—answers that all centered around pleading the blood of Jesus.

When you plead the blood of Jesus, you enter the holy of holies by the power and the virtue in that blood. Sin and death can't go there because they can't exist in the presence of God. You live in Jesus' righteousness. The knowledge of that truth begins to build up on the inside of you as you speak forth words of faith: "I'm living in the righteousness of God today. I'm walking in His footsteps today. The enemy cannot bring tragedy to my family. He cannot bring sickness or death to my home. God judges me the way He would judge Jesus. I'm pure and clean because of the blood of Jesus!"

And it doesn't stop there. God hasn't just provided the way for you to enter the holy of holies; He wants you to live there!

That's the key. After all, the presence of God resides on the inside of you. You don't have to live your life outside the holy of holies just because it's time to go to the grocery store. You and your children can live every aspect of your lives in God's presence. You never have to leave His presence—but it's only because of the blood of Jesus.

So what are you doing when you plead the blood of Jesus over yourself, your spouse and your children each morning? You are placing yourselves in the holy of holies, where the devil cannot come. He cannot cross that line, because on the other side of that line is the presence of God. The devil, his plans and devices are instantly destroyed!

That excites me so much, because in this day and the age in which we live, no physical location is a sanctuary. Schools are no longer sanctuaries. Even churches are no longer sanctuaries—unless the people understand how to build a hedge around their church by pleading the blood of Jesus.

There is only one true sanctuary, and that is before the throne of God. And it is God Himself who issues an invitation for us to draw near:

> Let us then fearlessly and confidently and boldly draw near to the throne of grace (the throne of God's unmerited favor to us sinners), that we may... find grace to help in good time for every need [appropriate help and well-timed help, coming just when we need it] (Hebrews 4:16 AMP).

This scripture is not talking about approaching the throne of grace once we get to heaven. We aren't going to need mercy for our failures after we go home to be with the Lord. All our needs and desires will already be met. No, this scripture is our promise for life on this earth.

So where is the help we need? Only in the holy of holies, at the throne of grace. By the blood of Jesus, we can approach God's throne with fearless confidence. That kind of bold confidence is what many of us have been missing—even those who know how to plead the blood. But, it is a necessary ingredient for living our entire lives in God's sanctuary, by faith.

Hearing Wisdom in the Holy of Holies

Living our lives in God's presence provides us with such a wonderful sense of security. That's where our answers are. That's where our wisdom is.

When my children were growing up, each morning when I prayed with them, we would plead the blood of Jesus over our lives. We charged our angels to go before us to protect us in all our ways. And, we added something else to our prayers. We also prayed for wisdom.

The Bible says that wisdom cries out (Proverbs 1:20). Well, I want my family to be in a position to hear God's wisdom when He speaks it to us. So, I say every morning,

"Wisdom cries out to us, and we listen and obey."

I find myself hearing the voice of God better when I live in the holy of holies—in His presence—every day, by the blood of Jesus. I make better decisions, and so do my children.

For instance, one day when my son, Max, was young, he came in and said about a certain brand of toys, "Mommy, I'm going to have to throw them all away. They don't honor God, and they don't further my ministry."

Now, I had been about to take those toys away from Max because I had been sensing in my spirit that they weren't good. But I didn't have to do that because my 8-year-old son heard wisdom from God—exactly what we had been praying for!

Max dwells in the holy of holies, even though at 8 years old, he didn't fully comprehend that. But while he was living in God's presence, he heard the Lord say to him, *That doesn't honor Me.*

My children have been trained to obey. So when Max heard that, he threw those toys away. He didn't think about how much they had cost him. He just threw them in the trash and left them there—and he hasn't regretted it a moment since.

As my children became teenagers, my desire to protect them and to know that they are able to hear wisdom grew in me. I was constantly talking to the Lord about them. I'm so glad they can live with Jesus in the holy of holies. That's where they will find wisdom. That's where the devil can't go to attack them.

When your children are in the presence of God, they are keeping company with the Wisdom of the ages. God will give them the wisdom to make right decisions about peer pressure, pornography, cigarettes, alcohol or premarital sex. Whatever the issue, God has wisdom for your children to protect them from the temptations of this world and the devil's evil strategies.

That divine wisdom resides in the holy of holies, and the only way your children can live there is by the blood of Jesus. When you and your children plead His blood, you enter the holy of holies, where God is ready to impart as much protection, favor and grace to you as He would to Jesus Himself.

As a parent, *you* must also hear wisdom in the holy of holies, if you want your children fully protected. There will be many times you will have to make decisions concerning your children and won't know for sure what to do. Thank God, you have His promise that He will give you wisdom liberally when you ask Him for it!

> If any of you is deficient in wisdom, let him ask of the giving God [Who gives] to everyone liberally and ungrudgingly, without reproaching or fault-finding, and it will be given him (James 1:5 AMP).

All you have to do is pray, "Lord, You said You would give me wisdom liberally and that I am to let Your peace rule and reign in my heart (Colossians 3:15 AMP). So I ask for wisdom and peace from You regarding the right way to go in this matter."

I can't remember a time when I prayed like that and didn't get an almost immediate answer from the Lord. One time, some people wanted one of my daughters to go somewhere with them, but I didn't have peace about it in my heart. I struggled with what to do because I didn't want to offend them.

I have found usually, we say we don't know what to do, when really, we just don't *want* to do it. But we need to lay aside the circumstances and the pressure and listen for God's wisdom to show us the way to go.

If you're listening to wisdom, none of those things matter. Your objective is to hear what God is trying to say to you so your children can stay protected and blessed. If you let the pressure of circumstances get to you, you may miss the voice of God.

Anyway, I talked to a friend about this situation with my daughter and told her, "I just don't know what to do."

"I bet you do know," she said.

"No, I don't," I protested.

"All right, then, ask God for wisdom," she replied.

So right there, I prayed, asking God for wisdom according to His promise in James 1:5. Then my friend said,

"Now, all circumstances aside, do you have peace about letting her go?"

"No, I don't," I answered.

There was the wisdom I needed! It was the answer the Holy Spirit had been trying to get across to me all along. But why was I finally able to hear wisdom when it had been crying out to me? Because I placed myself in a position to hear.

Wash Your Hands in Innocence

This helps us understand why the devil has been able to gain so much access to Christians in his strategies to steal, kill and destroy. Many believers haven't been living where they're supposed to be living!

You should make it your goal to abide in God's presence continually. His throne room should be your home.

In Psalm 26:6 AMP, the psalmist David gives us a better understanding of what is required to make the altar of God, the holy of holies, our home: "I will wash my hands in innocence, and go about Your altar, O Lord."

We saw earlier in Psalm 24:4 that we can only draw near to God with clean hands and a sincere, pure heart. We can't just act any way we want to and then expect to get away with it by pleading the blood. We have to live right and do the right things.

In Psalm 26:6 AMP, David makes the same point when he

says, "I will wash my hands in innocence." But how do we do this? By appropriating the blood of Jesus into our lives.

We are citizens of heaven—not of this earth. But it is only by washing ourselves with the blood of Jesus that we can plead innocent to the accusations of the enemy. Even though God has given us the ability to "go about His altar," living continually in His presence, we must get there by washing our hands in innocence through the cleansing blood of the Lamb.

In John 6:53-56, Jesus also speaks of eating His flesh and *drinking* His blood in order to dwell in Him. It must have been a real shock to the disciples when Jesus told them that! Think about it. They had been taught all their lives never to partake of blood. It was forbidden under Levitical law. But Jesus said, "For my flesh is meat indeed, and my blood is drink indeed. He that eateth my flesh, and drinketh my blood, dwelleth in me, and I in him" (John 6:55-56).

So how do we obey this unusual command from the Master? Consider the difference between drinking and bathing in water. When we bathe in water, we use it to cleanse ourselves. But when we *drink* water, we take it in, appropriating its refreshing properties to revive and bring new life to our bodies.

In the same way, we have been cleansed from sin by the blood of Jesus, but we shouldn't stop there. We must also "drink" it in—appropriating its life-giving, protecting power into every aspect of our lives. Just as we must partake of water every day in order to survive physically, we must do the same with the blood of Jesus to protect our children and ourselves.

Standing in the Protection of God's "Even Place"

Let's go back to Psalm 26 for a moment. In verse 12 AMP, David describes what life is like as he "goes about" the altar of God: "My foot stands on an even place; in the congregations will I bless the Lord."

What a promise God has given us in this verse! Our families can go through life standing on an even place. That's talking about the habitation of God's house—a secure sanctuary with no unexpected bumps to make us stumble and fall. That place is the holy of holies. Nowhere can we find a place more "even" or secure than that!

You may miss it and go over a bump of your own making. But even then, the Lord will see to it you and your family are protected as you apply the blood of Jesus to your lives.

God knows who you are, what you're up against, and that you are changing, day by day, into the image of His Son. He has made a way, through the blood of Jesus, for you to win as thoroughly as you would had you already been perfect!

Your family can win 100 percent of the time as you are faithful to keep them standing on that even place, through the power of the blood of Jesus.

David had no higher priority than to dwell in that even place all the days of his life. In Psalm 27:4 AMP, he said:

> One thing have I asked of the Lord, that will I
> seek, inquire for, and [insistently] require: that I
> may dwell in the house of the Lord [in His pres-
> ence] all the days of my life, to behold and gaze
> upon the beauty [the sweet attractiveness and
> the delightful loveliness] of the Lord and to
> meditate, consider, and inquire in His temple.

David had to go to a physical Temple in order to dwell in God's presence. But when Jesus died on the cross, the veil separating the holy of holies in the Temple was ripped open, and the Holy Spirit came out to dwell within God's people.

Now *we* are the temple of the living God (2 Corinthians 6:16). We can enjoy the sweetness and protection of His presence as we dwell in that even place by the blood of Jesus:

> The secret [of the sweet, satisfying companionship]
> of the Lord have they who fear (revere and worship)
> Him, and He will show them His covenant and

reveal to them its [deep, inner] meaning. My eyes
are ever toward the Lord, for He will pluck my feet
out of the net (Psalm 25:14-15 AMP).

God will pluck your family's feet out of the net the enemy
has laid for them. Why? Because your eyes are ever toward
the Lord. You are trusting Him for deliverance from the "day
of trouble" spoken of in Psalm 27:5 AMP:

For in the day of trouble He will hide me in His
shelter; in the secret place of His tent will He
hide me; He will set me high upon a rock.

When you plead the blood of Jesus, you are laying down
your pride and ability to protect yourself, your spouse and
your children. Instead, you are picking up the ability of God,
putting yourself in a position where God can move on your
behalf to hide you and your family from trouble.

Notice all these verses in Psalms talk about being protected as you stand continually in the presence of God. I'm
telling you, my friend, this is the key! You live in God's presence by daily pleading the blood of Jesus over yourself and
your family's lives in faith. As you do, you put your family in
a position to live each day in the sanctuary the devil can't
touch—the heavenly holy of holies!

We Have Our Part to Play

Now look at Hebrews 10:23 AMP:

> So let us seize and hold fast and retain without
> wavering the hope we cherish and confess and
> our acknowledgement of it, for He Who prom-
> ised is reliable (sure) and faithful to His word.

Notice again, even though we have full freedom to enter
the holy of holies, it isn't automatic. We must seize, obtain,
draw near, lay hold, enter in and hold fast to the eternal hope
we cherish, confessing and acknowledging what He has done
for us by pleading the blood of Jesus. Verse 23 also says He
who promised is "reliable (sure) and faithful to His word."
People say, "God is so faithful to His people!" This is certainly true, but this verse says God is faithful to *His Word*. In
a sense then, because His power is in His Word, as we are
faithful to and line up with it, we open the way for Him to
work mightily in our behalf.

God is faithful and always doing 100 percent of what we
allow Him to do for us. He can do very little for our finances,
for example, if we're speaking lack, and very little to protect
us if we're constantly speaking death. Thankfully, He endeavors
to teach us when we mess up, and He is truly the God of a
second chance (and a third and a fourth, etc.)! Even so, if we

want to live victorious lives we must speak, receive and appropriate His Word on a daily basis. If we'll be faithful to His Word, He will be fully faithful to us. When we speak what His Word says over the situations we face, He can fix things fast!

It is actually good news to know God has bound Himself to His Word. This means all we have to do is say what He says, and the outcome is assured! God will be faithful to perform in our lives what He has promised. He will meet our needs and protect our children. He will do what He says He'll do.

CHAPTER 5

The Absolute Certainty
of Divine Protection

∽೦ᴄ

Here is an absolute guarantee: There is no more certain place to be than in the presence of God. And when I say *certain*, I mean "safe, secure and assured." You can count on it! Even if the Lord were to prompt you to go minister to someone in a hospital filled with deadly, contagious diseases, for example, you could go with confidence and peace, knowing you would be walking in His presence, where there is certain, supernatural protection.

Hebrews 6:19 AMP talks about that hope which helps us enter the absolute certainty and security of God's presence:

[Now] we have this [hope] as a sure and steadfast anchor of the soul [it cannot slip and it
cannot break down under whoever steps out
upon it—a hope] that reaches farther and enters
into [the very certainty of the Presence] within
the veil.

Let's read the two previous verses to find out what that
hope is:

Accordingly God also, in His desire to show
more convincingly and beyond doubt to those
who were to inherit the promise the unchange-
ableness of His purpose and plan, intervened
(mediated) with an oath. This was so that, by
two unchangeable things (His promise and His
oath) in which it is impossible for God ever to
prove false or deceive us, we who have fled [to
Him] for refuge might have mighty indwelling
strength and strong encouragement to grasp and
hold fast the hope appointed for us and set
before [us] (verses 17-18 AMP).

Verse 17 is talking about the oath God made to Abraham,
the father of our faith. To show Abraham "convincingly and

beyond doubt" that what He had promised him was absolutely certain, God intervened with an oath made by blood. Thus, by those two unchangeable things—God's promise and His oath made by blood—we, too, can grasp and hold fast to the hope set before us.

Whenever the Lord says with great certainty in His Word that you can possess something, it should be very difficult for the devil to take that promise away from you. It may be harder to be confident if you are praying for something not specifically promised in the Word, but in that case, you need a strong inner knowing from the Holy Spirit that the petition you have asked for is yours to claim.

You are a covenant person. Therefore, you should be confident God will perform His promise of protection for you as you stand in His presence by faith.

God wants you to grasp the hope He has given you through His promise of protection. The blood of Jesus can work in your life so much more powerfully when you are fully persuaded.

You don't get very far when you are wavering in your faith, always wondering, *Is pleading the blood of Jesus going to accomplish anything? Are my children really going to be delivered in the midst of danger just because I do this every day?* That's why God wants you to be convinced beyond a shadow of a doubt that He will faithfully keep you and your children safe from all harm.

God laid out in His Word all the provisions of His covenant with us, including supernatural deliverance and protection. Then He swore an oath by the blood of Jesus, giving us the mighty indwelling strength and strong encouragement to firmly grasp hold of this hope that has been set before us.

Verse 19 AMP says this hope is a sure and steadfast anchor of the soul. The soul—made up of your mind, will and emotions—needs anchoring because it is the arena where the devil most often attacks. If it weren't for the battle in our thought lives and our roller-coaster emotions, it would be much easier to make our flesh fall in line with our spirit man. Therefore, the soul must be consciously and continually renewed and submitted to God and His Word.

For instance, as you live your daily life, fear or worry can attack your mind and cause you to waver from the Word. That's when you have to anchor your tumultuous emotions by telling your soul, "Be quiet! I'm acting according to what the Word of God says, not according to circumstances."

Your hope lies in the oath God made by the blood of His Son to perform every promise in His Word. You have that hope as a steadfast anchor for your soul. That hope cannot slip or break, no matter who tries to step on it. It's a hope that reaches far into your heart, into the very certainty of the presence of God within the veil. It is something you can literally lay your hands on and put into force, knowing with absolute certainty that God will do exactly what He said He would do for you, through the power in the blood of Jesus.

Nothing Missing, Nothing Broken

I want to go further into the Word to "prove my case" that God's promise to protect us from every calamity is certain and sure. Let's start by looking at Romans 5:1 AMP:

> Therefore, since we are justified (acquitted, declared righteous, and given a right standing with God) through faith, let us [grasp the fact that we] have [the peace of reconciliation to hold and to enjoy] peace with God through our Lord Jesus Christ (the Messiah, the Anointed One).

Paul uses a lot of legal words in this chapter. For example, in this verse he says we have been *justified* or "acquitted" before the Judge of all.

One of the biggest robbers of the Church today is in the making of excuses. When you make an excuse for the shape your life is in, you are trying to justify yourself. In so doing, you take your justification out of the hands of the only One who can actually *make* you righteous and blameless. You'll be excused all right—excused from protection and blessings!

When people go through a tragedy and say, "It must have been God's will," I believe that qualifies as an excuse. It puts all the responsibility on God. It excuses the person from taking any responsibility, and denies the possibility they may have failed to fulfill a divine requirement. So much of God's power is forfeited in living this way because there is no allowance for His justification. Don't make that same mistake! Do whatever you have to do to grasp the fact that you have peace with God to hold and enjoy—He wouldn't bring that tragedy on you! (By the way, have you noticed God often uses words like "grasp" and "hold," as in the previous verse? These truths are really something He wants us to get hold of!)

Let's look at the root meaning of the Hebrew word *shalom*. Learning this from Billye Brim has forever changed the way I read God's Word! *Shalom* means "nothing missing, nothing broken." Those few words speak volumes. *Peace* then, is literally living with nothing missing and nothing broken in your life. That's God's way. He has given you and your family everything you could ever need or require to be completely whole and successful in life.

Everything you need to accomplish all God has ever asked you to do, has been set aside in abundance for your peace and wholeness. There should never be a time when you or your family members are not whole. But how do you reach that place of peace and wholeness? Only by the blood of Jesus.

If you look throughout God's Word, you will see that

wherever things were missing, God replaced them with better things. Wherever things were broken, He fixed them or gave something brand new.

That's what God wants to do for you, as well. By the blood of Jesus, you have peace and total reconciliation with Him. He will guard and guide you and your family in every area of life so nothing is ever left missing or broken. Regardless of the calamities that may befall the earth—the shootings, bombings, airplane crashes, earthquakes and tornadoes—God says, "Grasp firmly the peace you have with Me through the blood of My Son. Nothing need ever be broken or missing in the lives of you or your family."

Divine Protection:
More Certain Than Being Born Again?

It's easy to say, "Oh, I do believe God will protect my family from all harm." But you need to be so sure of that fact that you immediately respond in faith when your family is attacked by the enemy.

How can you be that certain of God's protection? Let's read on in Romans 5:2 AMP:

Through Him also we have [our] access (entrance, introduction) by faith into this grace (state of

> God's favor) in which we [firmly and safely]
> stand. And let us rejoice and exult in our hope
> of experiencing and enjoying the glory of God.

Through Jesus we have access into the holy of holies. We stand firmly and safely in this state of God's favor and grace. It is a place where no matter what the devil tries to do, God looks at us and says, "I judge you the way I would judge Jesus. I see you as possessing all the good qualities Jesus possesses. I am just as ready to move on your behalf as I am ready to move on the behalf of My Son."

That's what happens when you stand in God's grace and favor. As Isaiah 54:17 says, no weapon formed against you will prosper in that place because you, by virtue of His righteousness, stand firmly and safely in the sanctuary of His presence.

But your access into God's presence is by faith. That means you have to exercise your faith. You have to aggressively lay hold of your right to enjoy continual access to God's throne just because the Word says it is true.

Now let's look at what verse 9 AMP says:

> Therefore, since we are now justified (acquitted,
> made righteous, and brought into right relation-
> ship with God) by Christ's blood, how much

more [certain is it that] we shall be saved by
Him from the indignation and wrath of God.

First of all, let's see what Paul is referring to in this verse
when he says "the indignation and wrath of God."

Paul is talking about the judgments that come as a
result of sin on this earth. God is 100 percent against sin.
But although His wrath against sin will one day be poured
out, that isn't happening now. When it does, people will
definitely know it! However, we, as believers, won't be here
to see it.

So what is Paul talking about when he says we will be
saved from the indignation and the wrath of God? He is
saying that God will deliver us from paying the price for
sin—which is death. That would include all the devil could
bring against you.

Now let's look at the profound statement this verse
makes about how certain God's covenant promise of protection is for you and your family. Paul says your assurance
should be so certain God will deliver you from dangerous
situations, tragedy, loss, sickness, disease—or anything else
the enemy might throw at you—it even exceeds the absolute
certainty that He has saved you from sin in the first place!

Let's see what else the Word says about this.

> For if while we were enemies we were reconciled
> to God through the death of His Son, it is much
> more [certain], now that we are reconciled, that
> we shall be saved (daily delivered from sin's
> dominion) through His [resurrection] life
> (Romans 5:10 AMP).

If God would deliver you while you were still His enemy, wouldn't He do even more for you now that you're His child?

Suppose I asked you, "Are you certain you're saved?"

You would probably say, "Well, of course, I'm saved!"

"Well, I don't know. I don't really think you're saved."

"Yes, I am!" you'd say indignantly. "I'm going to heaven. Jesus is my Lord."

More than likely, you are that certain you are a child of God. But, as you can see, according to this scripture, you should be that much *more* certain God will daily deliver you and your children from sin's dominion than you are in your confidence that you are saved!

But what is "sin's dominion"? It is the judgment or the price attached to sin. That includes all tragedies, killings and natural disasters that take place on this earth. It includes poverty, train wrecks, car accidents and every sickness and disease.

All these things fall under the category of sin's dominion because the wages of sin is death. God has provided a way to deliver you from judgment through the blood and resurrection life of His Son. And He says He will daily deliver you and your children from them *all*. That should be an absolute certainty in your heart. There should be no question about it. Because of the blood of Jesus and His righteousness, you don't deserve the dominion or the recompense of sin. The devil should never be able to come in and convince you that God is not going to protect your family. You have God's Word on it, and it is impossible for Him to lie.

A Way of Escape

We have established as an absolute certainty that God will protect and deliver us from sin's dominion. It thrills me every time I think about it! So many of us have thought we were still subject to unexpected tragedies and calamities. We *hoped* God would protect us, but it wasn't all that certain to us.

But now we're beginning to see how the grace of God works to bring us divine protection. Grace is able to work for us because we're in the footsteps of Jesus. We stand in His righteousness. It has nothing to do with our own goodness or righteousness. (If you didn't lead a very righteous life in the past, that's probably very good news to you!)

Verse 12 AMP goes on to describe where we all were before God made a way of escape for us through Jesus:

Therefore, as sin came into the world through
one man, and death as the result of sin, so death
spread to all men, [no one being able to stop it
or to escape its power] because all men sinned.

Before Jesus, sinful people didn't have a way to escape
the power of death except for the temporary fix God put into
place through animal sacrifices. But now, there is a way of
escape. We can escape every form of sin and death at work in
the earth today through the blood of Jesus.

Death Will No Longer "Hold Sway"

One day I was studying the Word on the blood of Jesus,
and the Lord caught my attention with the first part of
Romans 5:14 AMP. It says, "Yet death held sway from Adam
to Moses...."

Death held sway from Adam to Moses.... That phrase
caught my eye. I didn't know what it meant, so I thought, *I
know! I'll call my dad.*

My dad, Kenneth Copeland, is my ever-ready "Bible encyclo-
pedia." But when I called him, I found out he had gone fishing!

Since I couldn't ask Dad, I thought, *I guess I'll just have to
ask the Lord.* (The Lord is the One I should have asked in the
first place!)

I said, "All right, Lord, what does this mean? You obviously want to tell me something."

To my surprise, the Holy Spirit answered me immediately with one simple word: *Passover*.

Death did hold sway from Adam to Moses. But on the night of that first Passover, it lost its control.

Before the first Passover, death held the cards, so to speak. No one could escape its power. Everything on this earth was going death's way. It held sway until that night when God's people applied the blood of the Passover lamb to their doorposts. Death could no longer push its way in where it didn't belong. It had to pass over the Israelites' homes that were protected by the blood.

The same thing is true today. Death still holds sway in the lives of people who don't know the Lord. But if you do know Him, the Lamb of God shed His blood for you and your family. And if you'll just apply it to the doorposts of your life by pleading the blood, death has to pass over.

Imagine What It Was Like

Take a moment to imagine yourself in the days when the children of Israel were in slavery. See yourself and your family there the night Moses said the Lord would lead His people out of bondage.

You pick up the hyssop branch and apply the blood of the Passover lamb to your door and its side posts, just as God commanded Moses. The blood is on your doorposts, and you, your spouse and your children are gathered together behind that door. You hold your youngest child in your arms.

You know your sister is in her home down the street. Her family has also applied the blood of their Passover lamb to their door.

You and your family are sitting together at the table, recounting what God has done for your people in the past, enjoying your time together behind the door of your home. All of a sudden, you begin to hear weeping and crying. Children are dying in their mothers' arms. Those mothers wail, "Oh, my baby, my baby!" but there is nothing they can do except cry in agony.

The screams are horrendous. All that horror and grief is right on the other side of your door. Every member of your family can hear the effects of death outside.

Then you look around the room at your own family, and know with unshakable certainty they will come through this night unscathed, unharmed and secure. There is no question or doubt in your mind about it. You don't have one moment of fear or anxiety, wondering what might happen to your children.

You realize that because of the promise God gave you—because you obeyed His instructions to put that blood on your doorposts—death cannot come into your home. It is going to pass over.

You look at your little baby snuggled contentedly in your arms, and know this little one is protected. You look at your children and your spouse sitting around the table, and know they're safe from all harm. Death may surround you, but it can't touch you or your family because of the blood of the Passover lamb.

What security, what peace—what "blessed assurance"!

But think about it—that's just a fraction of what we have in Jesus today. The children of Israel were delivered from death by the blood of an animal. But as the Word says, how much *more* does the blood of Jesus deliver us from every form of sin's dominion? (See Hebrews 9:14.)

Today, we see mothers crying on television newscasts because their children have died. We see people wailing in grief over the loss of their loved ones during an earthquake or a hurricane. To the world, none of these tragedies make any sense. They seem inescapable.

But thank God, we don't live in "the land of Egypt"! There is light in "the land of Goshen." We live behind the blood of Jesus in the holy of holies. That precious blood protects us and delivers us from all evil. All we have to do is daily apply the blood of Jesus with our words, to the doorposts of our lives.

As we learn to appropriate and honor the blood of Jesus,

we and our families will be able to walk through life just as certain of our protection as the Israelites, when they sat behind their blood-stained doorposts and death passed them by.

The Blood of Jesus Seals Us in God's Grace

The Israelites could have chosen to open their doors and go outside on that Passover night. Had they done that, they still would have been God's people. But because the blood of the Passover lamb represented the propitiation, or the atonement, for their sin, in leaving their homes, they would have put themselves outside the protection of that blood, where death *could* go after them.

The Hebrew word meaning "propitiation" or "atonement" doesn't just mean to cover sin. The root word actually refers to bitumen or pitch, a substance akin to the tar Noah used to seal and waterproof the Ark.[3]

The pitch covering Noah's Ark sealed out the rain and sealed the occupants of the Ark inside God's protection. In the same way, the blood of Jesus doesn't just cover sin, it actually acts as a seal between us and sin. It seals sin out and seals us in the grace of God.

---

3 James Strong, *Hebrew Dictionary of the Old Testament, The New Strong's Exhaustive Concordance of the Bible* (Nashville: Thomas Nelson Publishers, 1985), #3722.

The blood of Jesus seals you and your family inside the holy of holies with all the good things of God. At the same time, it seals out all the bad things the devil wants to throw at you.

Let's go back to an earlier passage in Romans for a moment. I want to show you a picture of the world as we know it today. It is a very fitting description of what the blood of Jesus has sealed us from.

It is so funny to me when people talk about the "irrelevance" of the Bible. They must not know what it says. The truth is, the Word of God is always current. Just look at what Romans 3:10-18 AMP says:

> As it is written, None is righteous, just and truthful and upright and conscientious, no, not one. No one understands [no one intelligently discerns or comprehends]; no one seeks out God. All have turned aside; together they have gone wrong and have become unprofitable and worthless; no one does right, not even one! Their throat is a yawning grave; they use their tongues to deceive (to mislead and to deal treacherously). The venom of asps is beneath their lips. Their mouth is full of cursing and bitterness. Their feet are swift to shed blood. Destruction [as it dashes them to pieces] and misery mark their ways. And

they have no experience of the way of peace [they know nothing about peace, for a peaceful way they do not even recognize]. There is no [reverential] fear of God before their eyes.

That is such a good description of the world today! People in the world think they have the answers and that Christians are foolish. But the truth is, worldly people are the ones who are foolish—so foolish, in fact, they don't even recognize the truth when they see it!

This passage describes the perilous road to judgment. But, praise God, we can get off that road! We don't have to be there when judgment is taking place. And if we are in a place where it is happening, we don't have to be part of it. We are not citizens of the world as this passage describes. We are citizens of heaven, sealed in the grace of God through the blood of Jesus!

Now let's read verses 21-26:

But now the righteousness of God [or the ability to stand in God's presence in the Holy of Holies] without the law is manifested, being witnessed by the law and the prophets; even the righteousness of God which is by faith of Jesus Christ unto all and upon all them that believe: for there is no difference: for all have sinned, and come short of the glory of God; being justified freely by his grace through the redemption that is in Christ Jesus: whom God hath set forth to be a propitiation [a cover or a seal] through faith in his blood, to declare his righteousness for the remission of sins that are past, through the forbearance of God; to declare, I say, at this time his righteousness: that he might be just, and the justifier of him which believeth in Jesus.

If you want Jesus to be your Justifier, you must declare with the words of your mouth that because of His blood He is your Justifier. He will then *be* your Justifier—the One who declares you are innocent by His blood.

The blood of Jesus paid for your righteousness. Therefore, your justification—the right to live in the holy of holies, safe from the effects of judgment on this earth—is accomplished only through faith in His blood.

Stay in Your Sanctuary

We have a sanctuary that is far more powerful than the blood of the Passover lamb that was put on the Israelites' doors. We have a sure and certain sanctuary in the powerful blood of Jesus.

Doesn't it just thrill you to know about the power in the blood of Jesus? In this age of uncertainty you may be sure of what you're going to do each day, but who knows what the person driving the car next to you or the person walking into the post office behind you is going to do?

Praise the Lord! It doesn't matter what anyone else does—you can live in your sanctuary. No matter what kind of situation you may find yourself in, just stay in that sanctuary. Wherever your children go, keep them safe within that sanctuary. Teach them to stay in the holy of holies. God will even help them pick their friends. He will see to it they are protected and where they need to be.

Come boldly before God's throne by virtue of the blood. Walk in the footsteps of Jesus into the holy of holies, and ask for righteous judgment. No matter what is going on all around you, fix your heart on the certainty of God's protection as you plead the blood of Jesus over your family every day. Chaos and judgment may swirl just outside your door, but you and your children will stay safe in your sanctuary, protected by the blood of the Lamb!

Keep Your Heart Fixed

Psalm 112:7-8 AMP describes someone whose heart is fixed on God and His Word, a person who is absolutely certain of his protection within the sanctuary of God:

> He shall not be afraid of evil tidings; his heart is firmly fixed, trusting (leaning on and being confident) in the Lord. His heart is established and steady, he will not be afraid while he waits to see his desire established upon his adversaries.

This really describes my family during those times the enemy has tried to come against us. We truly are not afraid of evil tidings.

I don't say that in a prideful way at all; it's just the truth. For instance, my daughter Jenny was in a car accident when she was 18 months old. Paramedics said she was unresponsive at the scene and they didn't expect her to make it. But the Lord supernaturally delivered Jenny. In just a few days, she was out of the hospital!

How did that happen? While at the hospital, we kept our hearts fixed on God's covenant promises and the power of the blood. Instead of yielding to fear, we waited to see our desire established on our enemy, the devil. We knew what the outcome would be because our blood covenant with God made us secure.

The blood of Jesus was shed for your salvation and deliverance from sin's dominion. It is your faith in the Word of God and the blood of Jesus that makes you unafraid when challenges arise. You can do anything God asks you to do. You can go anywhere God asks you to go—as long as you are certain of your covenant with Him.

Since Jenny's accident, my family has learned so much more about applying the blood of Jesus to our lives. Today we are much further ahead of where we were spiritually when that happened.

Too many Christians react in fear to any kind of evil tidings. They are not covenant-minded. When bad things happen, they become fearful that something similar will happen to them.

For instance, when a shooting occurred at a Fort Worth church, it scared a lot of Christians. They started asking, "If I can't send my kids to *church* and know they are protected, where *can* I send them?"

The truth is, you can't send your children anywhere and know for certain they'll be protected, unless you walk by faith in your covenant and in the blood of Jesus. On the other hand, if you live this way—if you become covenant-minded and learn to stay in your sanctuary by the blood of Jesus—your heart will become fixed. You will know beyond a shadow of a doubt that God's promise of protection is not a vague hope, but an established fact.

By contrast, Psalm 112:10 AMP describes the way a person who doesn't know the Lord responds to adversity:

The wicked man will see it and be grieved and angered, he will gnash his teeth and disappear [in despair]; the desire of the wicked shall perish and come to nothing.

Have you ever seen unsaved people deal with a difficult situation the way this verse describes? I have. For instance, I have watched the different reactions of unsaved parents whose children were ill with a terminal disease. Some of them were very angry, some were upset; and some just sat in despair with no clue about what to do. They just waited for the doctor to tell them what was going to happen to their child.

Lacking a Savior, these parents had no recourse but to accept whatever the enemy would throw at them. Put this scripture together with Proverbs 12:13, which says that the wicked is snared by the transgression of his lips. He has an evil heart of unbelief. When something tragic occurs, what can he do? He will see it (the evil tidings) and be grieved and angry, but his desire for deliverance will come to nothing. He is without hope and without God in the world, as it says in Ephesians 2:12.

On the other hand, the covenant man's desire is to see his adversary, the devil, defeated. He just waits, expecting to see his desired outcome. He knows it is coming and is confident that he stands in a place of favor and grace before the throne of God. His heart is fixed.

Does that describe you? If you can't answer with a confident yes, it's time to work on becoming a covenant-minded believer! Fix your heart on the Word and on the power in the blood of Jesus until all doubts in your mind are erased forever. No matter what is going on around you, keep your family in the sanctuary of God's presence by pleading the blood of Jesus every day.

Remember, there is no more certain place to be than in the presence of God—secure in your covenant with Him.

CHAPTER 6

It's Your Choice!

❦

Now that you know about the certainty of God's promise of protection, you can probably understand better what I'm about to tell you: It's entirely your choice whether or not your family is protected.

The world may tell you otherwise. Even certain religious people will tell you it is God's choice—not yours—whether or not your family is protected from harm. But that just isn't what God's Word says. You have a big part to play in ensuring that you and your children dwell safely in God's sanctuary.

Do Martyrs Have a Choice?

As I have gone from place to place teaching on this subject of protecting your family by the blood of Jesus, one question people have asked me is this: "If those who were martyred through the years couldn't choose to be protected from physical harm and death, why can we choose?"

I thought that was a good question, so I began praying about it. "What about that, Lord?" I asked. "Why can we choose to be protected, yet the martyrs couldn't choose the same thing?"

The Lord led me to Hebrews 11 for my answer. I had read this chapter many, many times before. I knew it was the "hall of faith," the chapter where God talks about the faith exploits of the mighty men and women of the Bible. But this time, I saw something I had never seen before. Let me show you what I mean:

> And what shall I more say? for the time would fail me to tell of Gedeon, and of Barak, and of Samson, and of Jephthae; of David also, and Samuel, and of the prophets: who through faith subdued kingdoms, wrought righteousness, obtained promises, stopped the mouths of lions, quenched the violence of fire, escaped the edge of the sword, out of weakness were made strong, waxed valiant in fight, turned to flight the armies of the aliens (Hebrews 11:32-34).

This sounds familiar, doesn't it? It sounds like some of the violence going on in the world today! Back then, people faced swords and wild lions. Today, people face other dangers.

If the writer of Hebrews had lived in modern times, he might have said, "They quenched the violence of gunfire and escaped the threat of bombings and terrorists." These are the types of modern perils we want our children to be delivered from. We want to know they're continually protected from calamity and evil, no matter what may be happening around them.

Then verse 35 talks about those who were martyrs: "Women received their dead raised to life again: and others were tortured, not accepting deliverance; that they might obtain a better resurrection." Notice, it says these people were tortured because they didn't accept deliverance.

In other words, if martyrdom is what a believer wants, he can have that. The Bible says martyrs will have a better resurrection. But there is a lot to be said for walking in faith and accepting deliverance, too!

I want to make sure you understand I would never do or say anything to belittle a martyr's ultimate sacrifice for love of the Father. Anyone who would willingly give up his or her life for the gospel should be highly esteemed. God doesn't take the spilling of His people's blood lightly, and neither do I.

Make no mistake, I don't love my life more than I love God. I'm not afraid to die if given the choice to renounce Jesus or be killed. If someone were to point a loaded gun in my face and ask me if I loved Jesus, I would say without hesitation, "Yes, I love Jesus!" But according to this verse, it's my choice whether or not I am delivered from the death that could follow after taking that stand for the Lord—and I choose not to let someone take my life away from me!

We know from the writings of the early Church fathers that many of the saints of that time lived long, fruitful lives before choosing to be martyred. The Apostle Paul was one of them. His enemies couldn't kill him when they wanted to. He lived until he decided he had finished his course.

When death looked imminent, Paul even argued with himself about whether or not he wanted to go home to be with the Lord at that time. He told the Philippian church, "I'm torn between two desires: I long to go and be with Christ, which would be far better for me. But for your sakes, it is better that I continue to live. Knowing this, I am convinced that I will remain alive so I can continue to help all of you grow and experience the joy of your faith. And when I come to you again, you will have even more reason to take pride in Christ Jesus because of what he is doing through me" (Philippians 1:23-26 NLT).

Paul was actually debating within himself about whether or not he should lay down his life in martyrdom: Do I let them do this to me? Or do I stay here and keep working for the kingdom of God? He had a choice, and he knew it!

Why do you think Paul just slung off that poisonous

viper that had attached itself to his hand? (See Acts 28:3-5.) Because he had a choice. He knew it wasn't yet time for him to go to heaven, and he also knew his flesh wasn't subject to the dangers of the world. He knew he had a choice. So it was not a problem to him. He just flung off the viper and kept going about his business.

When Paul was an old man (in Philemon, he describes himself as being "Paul the aged"), he finally decided, "OK, I've finished my course now. It's time to go home." Only then was he martyred. Paul earned a martyr's crown, but also lived out his life until he knew he was finished with his divine assignment. Martyrdom was just the way he chose to go.

Just think what would have happened had Paul chosen martyrdom early in his life. We wouldn't have half the New Testament!

Remember, 1 John 4:17 says, "Herein is our love made perfect, that we may have boldness in the day of judgment: because as he is, *so are we* in this world." He said in John 10:17-18 that it was His choice whether or not He gave His life for mankind:

> Therefore doth my Father love me, because I lay down my life, that I might take it again. No man taketh it from me, but I lay it down of myself. I have power to lay it down, and I have power to

take it again. This commandment have I received
of my Father.

Jesus could have called 10,000 angels to deliver Him.
(According to 1 John 4:17, if He could have done that, so can
we!) He had a choice whether to pick up His life or lay it down.

Once you understand you have a choice, you can boldly
obey the Lord. You can go wherever He wants you to go and
do whatever He wants you to do. Even in the face of death,
you can keep your family safe. You can know you and your
children are protected because you have chosen to act on
your faith in the blood of Jesus.

Why Do Christians Get Caught
in Bad Situations?

Knowing you have a choice in this matter of divine protection may help you understand why Christians sometimes
get caught in bad situations. Seeing this happen many times
has a lot of Christians confused about whether or not they
can really trust God to protect *them*.

So let's talk about that. Why *do* Christians get caught in
bad situations? Well, first of all, let me say this one more
time: God's protection is not automatic. It would be if there
weren't an enemy trying to take it away from us every day.

God doesn't want us to have to struggle or work for the benefits He has provided for us, but we do have to be diligent to stand for and watch over in faith what belongs to us.

If the devil weren't out there, there would be no earthquakes, train wrecks, shootings or disease. Protection would be ours whether we exercised our faith in the blood of Jesus or not.

But the devil *is* out there, and never stops trying to take away our covenant blessings. That means we have to lay hold of our right to divine protection by standing in faith on God's Word and pleading the blood of Jesus over our families every day.

As an analogy, suppose you have hundreds of dollars in cash, and you decide to go walking through the worst part of town with some of that money hanging out in plain sight.

It's very likely you won't make it home with your money. Why? Because you didn't do anything to put yourself in a position of safety. You didn't properly secure your cash in a way that would protect it. Anyone who wanted it could come along, rip it out of your pocket and run off with it. The money would still be yours, but because you didn't protect it, you would lose out on its benefits.

That's a good picture of how we are to treat God's promise of protection. We have to choose to secure it by acting in faith on the power of the blood. Otherwise, the devil may come along and steal it from us.

Again, we need to understand that just because something happened doesn't mean it was God's will. God gave us His will. It is found in the pages of the Bible. But remember, that divine will isn't going to be fulfilled in our lives automatically.

Requirements for Protection

So what are the things God requires we do in order to escape the judgment present in this world? We must choose to follow His will, doing the things He says we must do to be protected and to live in obedience to His Word.

It is also important, as I mentioned before, to listen to our spirits, refusing to go where we're not supposed to be. And when we hear that small, quiet voice saying, *Don't do that*, we're supposed to listen and obey. This is so important to our own safety and to the safety of our children! We make things so much easier in our lives when we listen! As a mother, I'm always on the lookout for situations in which to teach this to my children.

Above all, we must take advantage of the power in the blood of Jesus, pleading His blood over our children every day. When we do this, we are building a hedge around our families through which judgment, death and tragedy cannot come.

First Peter 5:8 says, "Be sober, be vigilant; because your adversary the devil, as a roaring lion, walketh about, seeking whom he may devour." If you'll live according to these principles I've been sharing with you, you won't be one of those whom the devil can devour.

Satan is looking for people who aren't living according to their blood covenant with God—people whose ears are not open to His voice. Those are the devil's favorite kind of people! I think he likes passive Christians more than his own sinners. He knows he can blast those Christians' lives, steal their children, kill half of them and then convince them that it was all God's doing. The devil gets a perverse pleasure out of that strategy! He hates God and he hates you.

But Satan isn't going to get any pleasure out of my family! We are off-limits to him. I have already determined that no calamity will befall our home. I have laid hold of the power in the blood, and you can do the same for your family!

Build Up the Covenant Inside You

Many times as you plead the blood of Jesus on a daily basis, the circumstances surrounding you will change. But more than anything else, the practice of pleading the blood changes *you*.

Pleading the blood, however, isn't some magical incantation you do to keep the devil from hurting your family! It's the way you lay hold of God's promise of protection. As you plead the blood of Jesus, you are fortifying your spirit with words of faith and making your stand against the devil. You are changing your thought processes and solidifying and building up your covenant with God on the inside. That firm foundation in His love drives out fear.

Then, even when the devil tries to strike with one of his strategies against you or your family, you react the way the Word tells you to. You immediately speak deliverance according to the blood covenant you have with God.

Make it your goal to become covenant-minded in every area of life. Begin to see every obstacle you face through the eyes of your blood covenant.

For instance, if your child becomes sick, don't just see him through the eyes of your mind, will or emotions. If you do, your child will stay sick. Instead, respond according to the covenant you have with God. That covenant will reflect light on the situation, and you'll suddenly say, "Hey, this is not in my covenant with God! Jesus purchased my child's healing with the stripes on His back and with His blood! I claim total healing for my child's body in the Name of Jesus!"

That's why the heart of a covenant-minded believer is fixed as in Psalm 112, no matter what challenges may arise in life. His eyes are on the covenant and not on the situation. He knows his covenant says God will deliver him, so he just stays in faith, pleads the blood of Jesus and waits to see the outcome of his desire on the enemy.

When you plead the blood of Jesus every day, you are building the covenant strongly and solidly on the inside of you.

Then, when the pressure is on and you find yourself or your loved ones in a difficult situation, God's Word, our blood covenant, is what comes out of your mouth to deliver you.

For instance, I know of a covenant-minded woman who was in a bank when it was held up by thieves. The bank robbers made the people lie on the floor, then put guns to their heads and methodically began to shoot them one by one.

But when one of the robbers came to this woman, she boldly said, "The blood of Jesus is against you!"

The man snarled, "I don't know what's going on, but I can't shoot you!" Then he moved on to the next victim and continued his horrible task.

Long before this tragedy occurred, that woman had been building the covenant on the inside by making a practice of pleading the blood of Jesus. And when death stared her in the face, it was her choice to be delivered.

It's your choice as well. It's also your children's choice. If your teenager ever found himself in a situation where someone at school stuck a gun in his face and asked if he loved Jesus, he could say, "I plead the blood of Jesus!" He could choose to be delivered.

But that kind of faith-filled response doesn't come just because your child has heard about the blood of Jesus once in a while in a Sunday-school teaching. It comes after you have helped him build a solid foundation of the blood covenant in his heart and have pled the blood of Jesus over him day after day after day.

Every night in our home when my children were growing up, I pled the blood over them as I tucked them in. Then they prayed. Their prayers were every bit as powerful as mine. They would say, "I plead the blood of Jesus. No weapon formed against me shall prosper!"

My children know how to plead the blood. Their protection is very real to them. They built the blood covenant strong on the inside when they were young. And, should they ever be alone when faced with an attack of the enemy, that covenant will come out of their mouths to deliver them and keep them safe!

A Testimony of Deliverance by the Blood

I can speak from personal experience about the value of building the blood covenant on the inside of you before a demonic attack hits your family. On Christmas Day in 1995, my then 11-year-old daughter Lyndsey was struck, out of the blue, with an aggressive case of meningitis. One day she was fine, and then, suddenly, she was very, very sick.

Meningitis is a very fast-acting disease. Many times a child can be happily playing in the morning and be dead within 24 hours. The antibiotics don't have a chance to work because the parents are unaware the child is seriously ill until he is within minutes of dying.

Lyndsey started feeling sick with flu-like symptoms on Christmas Eve. By Christmas morning, she was feeling so sick she didn't want to come downstairs and open presents. I prayed over her and then went downstairs to share Christmas with the rest of the family. We didn't know Lyndsey was dangerously ill.

Then about 12:30 in the afternoon, a screeching cry came from Lyndsey's bedroom. We ran upstairs and found her screaming and thrashing on her bed, delirious. She didn't recognize anyone. Mystified, I thought, *Well, she was vomiting last night. Maybe her electrolytes are off.*

We called the doctor, and he said, "Take her to the hospital right away." By the time we arrived there, Lyndsey was totally unconscious. Her pupils were fixed and dilated, and she was as white as a sheet.

The medical staff took one look at her and rushed her past all the waiting patients into the emergency treatment area. They conducted a spinal tap, a procedure that entails taking fluid from the patient's spinal column. If the fluid is clear, it indicates good news for the patient. If it's cloudy, it means antibodies to fight meningitis are present, indicating the person has the disease.

I was standing near the doctor when he showed Lyndsey's spinal fluid to a nurse who remarked, "That's the cloudiest fluid I've ever seen!" That was a frightening thing for a mother to hear about her little girl!

The doctor then turned to me and said solemnly, "Your daughter has meningitis."

As soon as the doctor spoke those words, I felt as if someone had thrown a blanket of fear over me. That is the only way I know how to describe it. As that spirit of fear came on me, I could literally feel it trying to paralyze my own spirit.

Instead of responding to the doctor's words, I just turned around and left the room. He may have thought I was nuts, but right then I didn't know or care what anyone thought.

At that time, I didn't really know what meningitis was. I had read in the newspaper several instances of children contracting the disease in the area over the past couple of months, and knew those children had died. Although I didn't know how far the disease had developed in Lyndsey, I could see the doctors were treating her with an air of intense urgency.

When I walked out into the hall, my sister came to me and asked, "What is it?"

But before I could answer her, there was something I had to do. Let me point out here that I was not operating in the mental realm. Because I was living in the holy of holies I was responding out of my spirit in God's wisdom. I said, with a determined force that came from within, "I refuse fear!" Immediately, that blanket of fear lifted and left as if it were a whipped puppy. From that point on, I was able to operate on God's terms—not on fear's terms. Thank God for my parents who taught me to never let fear have its way!

Then I said, "Jesus, there is blood between me and You over Lyndsey. I have a covenant!"

For the rest of the ordeal with Lyndsey, I never had to deal with that kind of fear again. If a fearful thought tried to enter my mind, I was able to easily brush it away.

Later, everyone said, "Oh, you must have been terrified!" But I wasn't. I had total confidence the Lord would deliver my daughter.

Why was it that easy for me to deal with fear in such a life-and-death situation? Well, Lyndsey got sick about two and a half years after my cousin Nikki died. For those two and a half years, I had been daily pleading the blood of Jesus over my family, building the covenant strongly in my spirit.

I truly believe it was those two years of pleading the blood of Jesus that prepared me for this crisis. Because the covenant was so established in my heart, the enemy was defeated. I am so thankful God lets us know what we need before we need it!

If I had responded as do people of the world, my daughter would have gone the way of that disease and died. But because I knew I am not of this world—because I had built a hedge around my children with the blood—God was able to heal and deliver Lyndsey completely.

Declaring my covenant in that time of trouble was not something I had thought up beforehand. There wasn't time to run and grab some teaching CDs and read the Word to get strong in my spirit. What is inside you will come out in an emergency—good or bad. The reality of my covenant with God rose up on the inside of me and armed me for the battle.

I didn't know all I know now about the blood, but what I did know had changed me. Every day for more than two years, I had reaffirmed my faith in the covenant, pleading the blood of Jesus and speaking God's promises for my family. That daily exercise of reminding myself and the enemy that my family was covered by the blood had built the covenant strongly inside my spirit. When I needed that covenant to take effect, it rose up and determined the words of my mouth, causing me to do and say the right things when it mattered most.

I didn't have to stand there and think, *OK, now, what am I supposed to say and do in a situation like this?* In fact, because your mind shuts down in an emergency (Praise God!), you can't do that. This is a perfect example of Matthew 12:34-35.

> Oh generation of vipers, how can ye, being evil, speak good things? for out of the abundance of the heart the mouth speaketh. A good man out

of the good treasure of the heart bringeth forth good things: and an evil man out of the evil treasure bringeth forth evil things.

When you are under pressure, what's inside you will come out. If the Word isn't in you when trouble comes, it won't come out.

The blood covenant within me literally propelled those words of faith out of my mouth without my having to think about it at all. I love *The Amplified Bible's* version of verse 35. It says, "The good man from his inner good treasure flings forth good things." Well, my spirit started flinging! That disease had no right to my daughter's body!

At about 3:30 in the afternoon, the doctor started Lyndsey on strong antibiotics. However, he warned us not to get our hopes up. "Meningitis is very deadly," he told us. "We have antibiotics to fight the disease, but these antibiotics take at least 24 to 48 hours to have any kind of effect, and children who have contracted meningitis usually die before 24 hours have passed."

Remember, Lyndsey started feeling sick on Christmas Eve, so she had already been sick for 24 hours. That meant by the time we reached the hospital, the disease had almost reached the final stages of a process that normally ended in death.

I was quickly learning what a fast-acting, evil disease

meningitis is. All sickness and disease is evil, but this one has the devil's signature all over it. People who contract the disease and survive can lose hearing, limbs—even mental ability.

According to the doctor, something had to change quickly in Lyndsey's condition or she would die. When I calmly told him Jesus died on the cross so Lyndsey didn't have to die from this disease, he looked at us and said, "I can agree with that." I am sure he didn't know what he was saying, but God caused him to be in agreement.

This brings up another important point. When people are not established in their covenant, they are afraid of a doctor's report. Remember Psalm 112? Even Christians can fall into this category of the wicked if they have an evil heart of unbelief. I've seen people yell at the doctor, telling him they won't receive that report—then launch into their confessions and hurl them in his face.

What's the problem here? The problem (and the killer) is they're not doing these things out of faith in their covenant with God, but out of fear it won't work this time. All they get is an angry doctor and a firmer foundation of fear. You can't wage spiritual warfare out of fear, nor can you operate in fear and faith simultaneously. Fear and faith take up the same spiritual space.

About 8:00 that evening, Jerry and Carolyn Savelle came to the hospital to be with us (my parents were out of town at the time). While a family member stayed with Lyndsey, I went with the Savelles and my sister and brother-in-law (who are our pastors), to the hospital chapel to take Communion. I wanted to settle the matter in my heart. I didn't know it at the time, but my parents were doing the very same thing at the very same minute over 800 miles away!

We weren't trying to be religious or to impress God by taking Communion. We were remembering that Jesus shed His blood to bring our blood covenant with God to pass. So we set the scriptures before us that promised Lyndsey's healing. Then we partook of the Communion elements, knowing in our hearts she was well and whole because the Bible said it is so.

There is so much power in taking Communion! It seals your faith in the covenant you have already built up inside yourself by pleading the blood of Jesus each day.

As we sat there taking Communion, Jerry Savelle received a word from the Lord: *As suddenly as this has come on her, it is going to go.* When I left that chapel, there was no doubt in my mind we had won. No weapon formed against my daughter could prosper.

Before I could re-enter Lyndsey's room, I had to go through a complicated sterilization procedure, necessary because of the highly contagious nature of the disease. By the time I had put on all the hospital garb and carefully washed, about 15 minutes had passed.

When I was ready, I walked into Lyndsey's hospital

room—only to find her talking to the family member who was with her! When I had left to go to the chapel a short time before, she had been unconscious and delirious. To keep her from harming herself as she thrashed about, the medical staff had tied her to her bed.

Lyndsey hadn't been able to say a word that made sense from before we had gotten her to the hospital. It had been less than five hours since she had begun the antibiotics. Yet here she was, carrying on a conversation!

Overcome with joy, I asked, "What happened?"

I learned Lyndsey had been lying unconscious, but about 15 minutes before I'd entered the room she had turned her head and said to the family member, "Merry Christmas!" Then she had asked, "What are all these machines?"

Just that quickly, Lyndsey was in her right mind again. From that moment on, her recovery was miraculously rapid. It wasn't the antibiotics the doctor had given her because there hadn't been enough time for them to take effect. It was the healing power of God at work in my daughter's body that had turned the situation around.

By the time my parents had flown back home that evening, arriving at the hospital around midnight, Lyndsey was talking to all of us. She was having to use her faith for her head to stop hurting and for every symptom to go, but was well on her way back to complete wholeness.

The next morning, one of the doctors came in to check on Lyndsey and was shocked to see she was still alive, much less on her way to total recovery! The doctor had just seen the test results, which indicated Lyndsey had contracted the deadliest form of meningitis. Children just didn't live long after contracting this particular form of the virus.

It still had not been 24 hours since Lyndsey had been put on antibiotics. But at 8:00 that morning, she was ordered out of intensive care into a private room. I guarantee, only the blood of Jesus and the Word of God can do that!

Lessons Learned

I want to give you a few thoughts about what I learned through this situation with my daughter. First, one of the main passages of Scripture we stood on during the entire experience was Isaiah 54. As I mentioned before, there are some powerful covenant promises in that chapter. Let me show you just a few of them:

> And all thy children shall be taught of the Lord; and great shall be the peace of thy children. In righteousness shalt thou be established: thou shalt be far from oppression; for thou shalt not fear: and from terror; for it shall not come near thee. Behold, they shall surely gather together,

> but not by me: whosoever shall gather together
> against thee shall fall for thy sake. Behold, I have
> created the smith that bloweth the coals in the
> fire, and that bringeth forth an instrument for
> his work; and I have created the waster to
> destroy. No weapon that is formed against thee
> shall prosper; and every tongue that shall rise
> against thee in judgment thou shalt condemn.
> This is the heritage of the servants of the Lord,
> and their righteousness is of me, saith the Lord
> (verses13-17).

Verse 16 says, "I have created the waster to destroy." That doesn't mean God created the devil to destroy. We know from the Word that when God created Lucifer, he was perfect (Ezekiel 28:15). The literal Hebrew says that God created the waster *that* destroys, and He is saying in this verse, "I created him, and I can handle him."

God knows how to take care of the devil, and He is on our side. Therefore, we must give Him full freedom to thwart the enemy's attacks on our families and keep him out of our lives.

Isaiah 54:17 says, "Every tongue that shall rise against thee in judgment thou shalt condemn." Every day, the accuser of the brethren has his finger in your face, trying to condemn you with his evil judgments, such as, "You're sick. You're poor. I'm going to hurt your children today." But according to verse 17, we can condemn the devil's accusations against us. How? By pleading the blood.

These verses in Isaiah 54 were some of the scriptures I had used to build a covenant hedge of protection around our family for more than two years. We weren't standing in our own righteousness as we claimed these promises for Lyndsey. My family and I were standing in Jesus' righteousness by virtue of His blood. As we declared in faith that no weapon formed against Lyndsey would prosper, God delivered her from imminent death and restored her to total wholeness.

It wasn't because I am Kenneth and Gloria Copeland's daughter that God came through for Lyndsey. What made the difference is knowing who I am in Jesus and in His blood.

In the same way, it doesn't matter whether you are famous or unknown, or whether you are from a rich family or a poor one. A lot of money can get you a lot of things, but if you're sick there may be no earthly cure for your condition. You need to start doing things God's way. Money is a very poor source when it comes to healing, joy, peace or anything else, for that matter.

Finally, I want to share with you something else I learned through this whole situation. I discovered firsthand how God makes allowances for the times we miss it as we daily plead the blood of Jesus over our lives.

The Lord had been talking to me about taking Communion with my family on that particular Christmas

Eve. I had even bought all the Communion supplies to do it.

However, at the Christmas Eve family gathering, I was so busy enjoying our time together, I forgot what the Lord had told me to do. It wasn't until everyone was starting to leave that I remembered and said, "Oh, we forgot to take Communion." But because of the lateness of the hour and the fact that some family members were almost out the door, I decided, "Well, we'll just take Communion together next Christmas Eve."

That was a big mistake. After the entire ordeal with Lyndsey was over and she was back home again, the Lord spoke these words to my spirit: *If you had done what I said that night, you wouldn't have gone through this.*

God wasn't trying to start a new tradition in our family when He impressed me to take Communion together on Christmas Eve. He had a specific purpose for it. But I missed it when I took His prompting too lightly and decided to forego the family time of Communion for the sake of convenience.

My family could have bypassed that entire ordeal. We could have had a peaceful, healthy Christmas. Nevertheless, because I had faithfully pled the blood of Jesus over my family and built the covenant strong in my heart, God delivered my daughter out of a deadly situation. It ended up being a great Christmas after all.

You build a firm foundation for yourself when you plead the blood of Jesus every day. Then each day and month and year that you keep pleading the blood of Jesus, you put new layers on that foundation until the covenant is built solid and strong on the inside of you.

This is so important, because someday a devilish attack may come against you or your family like the one I faced with Lyndsey. In situations like that, you don't have time to get ready to take a stance of faith by meditating on some scriptures. You have to respond right the first time, or the devil wins the battle.

That's why you must keep building up the covenant in your spirit, pleading the blood of Jesus over your family day after day. Don't wait until problems arise to start building that covenant inside you. That would be like starting to build your house the night before a hurricane hits! No, you build a strong house on a solid foundation when it isn't storm season. Then, when the storm hits, nothing can knock it down.

It's the same way in the spiritual realm. If you have built a strong foundation of your covenant in your heart, you'll respond in the right way when pressure comes. Words of faith in God's covenant promises will come out of your mouth, bringing His power on the scene and giving you the victory.

You must choose to lay hold of your covenant of protection with God. The protection is there if you want it. It's your choice whether to get caught in a bad situation and let the enemy send you or your child on an early ride to heaven. Or you can lay hold of your protection by standing on God's Word and boldly plead the blood of the Lamb.

CHAPTER 7

It Matters Where You Live

❦

So, if it's your choice whether or not to be delivered, what is that choice hinging on? The answer is simple: It matters where you live. That's the key. Pleading the blood of Jesus will put you and your children in the place where you are supposed to abide continually—the holy of holies.

My friend, you make much better decisions when you live in that place. You hear God's voice better. You walk in love better. And when you plead the blood of Jesus in the morning, you secure your place there.

What You Say Is Where You Live

Remember what I told you earlier: Your faith in the blood is executed and entered into by the words of your mouth. Why is what you say so important? Because what you say is where you'll live.

If words of poverty, sickness and fear are coming out of your mouth, I guarantee you'll live in the natural realm with lots of poverty, sickness and fear. But if your words proclaim healing, prosperity and protection by the blood of Jesus, then you'll live in the holy of holies. Your natural circumstances may not have caught up with your confession of faith yet, but what you're saying is exactly where you're headed.

Look again at what Proverbs 12:13-14 AMP says about the connection between our words and divine protection:

> The wicked is [dangerously] snared by the transgression of his lips, but the [uncompromisingly] righteous shall come out of trouble. From the fruit of his words a man shall be satisfied with good....

"The wicked "referred to here is a person who isn't in covenant with God. However, the same principle applies to a person who doesn't *know* the covenant he has with God. Both will be dangerously snared by the transgression of their lips.

This explains why verse 21 AMP is true:

No [actual] evil, misfortune, or calamity shall
come upon the righteous, but the wicked shall
be filled with evil, misfortune, and calamity.

Think of these proverbs in light of what Moses said in
Deuteronomy 30:19:

I call heaven and earth to record this day against
you, that I have set before you life and death,
blessing and cursing: therefore choose life, that
both thou and thy seed may live.

It's very clear that where you live is your choice. You can
be one of the righteous who lives free from evil, misfortune
and calamity, or you can place yourself in the same category
as "the wicked" and live a life filled with evil, misfortune
and calamity.

Sadly, there are too many Christians living on that wicked
side of life—not because they want to be wicked or do evil
things, but because they don't say or do what God's Word
says. They don't honor the blood of Jesus, so their lives seem
to be filled with one crisis after another.

But these people don't have to live with calamity and
misfortune. They could choose to pick up their Bibles and
find out how to get out of their bad situations. They could

discover for themselves that things go well in the lives of those for whom the Word of God is the final authority!

The problem is that Christians who live on the wicked side of life don't give the Word any credence. "God didn't protect Grandma, so He won't protect me," they say. "Whatever happens is going to happen, and there is nothing I can do about it." And what they say is exactly where they end up living.

With that attitude, these Christians are not honoring the Word because God says there is something they *can* do about it. They can apply the blood of Jesus to their lives with their words.

Honor the Word

The key to living victoriously in this life is to become covenant-minded—to honor the blood of Jesus and the Word above everything else. That includes honoring the Word above your experiences, circumstances or what anyone else says. If your family doesn't agree with the Word of God, pray for them and walk in love with them, but always make sure you honor the Word.

I've counseled people who just couldn't seem to grasp this basic, all-important concept. One woman whom I've often counseled, comes crying to me with the same problem every time. At every counseling session, I sit down with her and ask, "Are you reading the Word?"

"Well, no," she replies. "I just..." and then gives me her latest excuse. Finally I told her, "Nothing is going to change in your life until you honor the Word and give it first place in your life. You have to come to the place where you say, 'My answers are in here, and I am determined to find them.'"

That's why God's Word talks so much about the man whose heart is fixed and established. He's the one who honors, reveres and worships the Lord (Psalm 112:7 AMP).

If you revere the Lord and put Him first place in your life, you'll go to His Word to find your answers. Then, whatever the Word says to do, you'll do it. You'll consider the Bible as your instruction Book for life.

That's what makes you a covenant person whose heart is fixed. Nothing can move you off your stance of faith. Death no longer holds sway in your life.

I think Ecclesiastes 12:13 AMP says it best:

> All has been heard; the end of the matter is: Fear God [revere and worship Him, knowing that He is] and keep His commandments [in other words, look to the Word as the end of all matters], for this is the whole of man [the full, original purpose of his creation, the object of God's providence, the root of character, the foundation of all happiness,

the adjustment to all inharmonious circumstances and conditions under the sun] and the whole [duty] for every man.

Notice what this verse says about the Word of God. For one thing, it is the root of character. As you immerse yourself in the Word and cement yourself in its truth, it becomes the root or the basis of your character. Character rooted in God's Word causes you to make the right choices and to do the right things. However, this kind of godly character is only developed when you make the Word the end of all matters in your life.

The Word of God is also the foundation of all happiness and the adjustment to all inharmonious circumstances and conditions under the sun. If you have an inharmonious circumstance or condition in your life, your answer will be found in God's Word. As you honor it and begin to seek wisdom in its pages, God will show you where your answer is.

There isn't one thing the enemy can throw at you or your family that you can't overwhelmingly overcome when you honor the Word above all else in your life. That means if the devil tries to attack your children, he can't leave them with anything missing or broken. Otherwise, he has prospered in his attack, and Isaiah 54:17 says that no weapon formed against you will prosper. Nothing Satan can come up with is bigger, higher or more powerful than the Word of God and the blood of Jesus that ratifies that Word.

Everything contained within the Bible was purchased for you by the blood of Jesus. Every promise in it belongs to you, and the devil can't do one thing about it, apart from what you allow him to do. He can't attack you or your children with any circumstance or condition that isn't answered in the Word of God.

You can overcome *every* demonic strategy against your family by honoring God's Word. Live by it, live on it, live in it. Remember—it matters where you live!

Learn how to live each day in the holy of holies by the blood of Jesus. Then when a challenge arises, come boldly before God's throne and ask Him to reveal to you in His Word, the answer you need.

Once you have your answer, make sure your words always stay in line with what God has said on the matter. Your words of faith will not only guarantee your ultimate victory, but will ensure you retain your current living status in the holy of holies.

Don't Be an "Earth-Inhabiter"

Revelation 12:10-12 has more to say about where believers are supposed to dwell during their lives on this earth:

> And I heard a loud voice saying in heaven, Now is come salvation, and strength, and the kingdom of our God, and the power of his Christ: for the accuser of our brethren is cast down, which accused them before our God day and night. And they overcame him by the blood of the Lamb, and by the word of their testimony; and they loved not their lives unto the death. Therefore rejoice, ye heavens, and ye that dwell in them. Woe to the inhabiters of the earth and of the sea! for the devil is come down unto you, having great wrath, because he knoweth that he hath but a short time.

Verse 12 tells us where we are today in God's timeline. In the past few years, tragic calamities have escalated more than ever before. We don't even live in the same world now that we did 20 years ago. The devil knows his time is short, and he is upset about it. He is desperate. Therefore, he is roaming the earth, trying to do everything he can to stop the inevitable victory of the Body of Christ.

What happens to you and your family depends on where you dwell. If you dwell in the heavens, in the holy of holies, God tells you to rejoice because you have overcome. You are one of those who comes boldly before the throne of grace by the blood of Jesus to receive everything you need.

But earth-inhabiters are going to experience calamities and misfortunes. The Bible says, "Woe to them!"

Too many children of God are still earth-inhabiters. That's why we're seeing so many good Christians taken out by the enemy through tragic circumstances. They become part of the earth-dwellers' woe because they choose to live their lives trusting in the world's system and in their own wisdom and ability. The devil has convinced them God won't protect them. The enemy has even succeeded in convincing some that God is their problem. They become earth-inhabiters, subject to the same calamities other people in the world suffer.

But the truth is, it's their choice. God's Word has the answers they need to become "holy of holies dwellers" and to overcome the enemy's strategies in their lives, if they would just choose to honor what He says above all else.

The Blood and Our Words

Verse 11 says heaven-dwellers overcome the enemy by the blood of the Lamb, and by the word of their testimony.

Notice there are two parts to this verse. As a heaven-dweller, you overcome the devil's strategies against your family by the blood of Jesus *and* by the word of your testimony.

As we have already discussed, nothing in the Word comes

without laying hold of it and speaking it forth in faith. When you were born again, you had to confess Jesus as your Savior. (See Romans 10:9-10.) In the same way, the blood of the Lamb won't deliver you unless you lay hold of it with the words of your mouth.

We know we are living in the last days. The earth is filling up with sin, judgment, tragedy and terrible circumstances because the wages of sin is death. However, Romans 5:20 says where sin abounds, God's grace much more abounds. According to that scripture, more grace is available to us now than ever before because sin is abounding more now than ever before.

The devil is mad. He knows his time is short and there isn't anything he can do about it. Therefore, he's plotting all sorts of evil things. Satan is going to try to take out as many people as he can, and Christians are the ones he would most like to get out of his way.

If you're not really doing anything to hurt the devil's kingdom, you might not be his main target. Nevertheless, you live on this earth where sin and judgment abounds more and more. That fact alone puts you in danger if you decide to be an earth-inhabiter.

But the devil isn't touching my family because we have decided to be kingdom-dwellers—not earth-inhabitors. Every morning we place ourselves under the protective covering of the blood of Jesus. We say, "We plead the blood of Jesus over our family this morning. Father, we dwell in the holy of holies today. We live our lives there. And we thank You, Lord, for the abundance of grace we find there to protect, deliver and meet every need!"

You can make that same choice. Instead of being earth-inhabiters, you and your children can be kingdom-dwellers—untouchable by the enemy because of the power in the blood of the Lamb.

Dwelling in the Secret Place

You should understand by now that you can live your life in absolute certainty that God will protect you and your children from harm, no matter what is going on around you. But let's look at another important passage of Scripture to make sure that knowledge is rooted deeply in your heart.

Psalm 91 is a chapter many Christians have stood on in faith at one time or another. But many of these same Christians think, *I've claimed that chapter for my family in times past, but it doesn't seem like we're living the full benefit of it. We haven't been delivered out of every attack of the enemy. Bad things have happened at times.*

Well, let's look a little closer at this chapter to find out why that is the case with so many Christians. Before we read it, however, let me stress again these two points: 1) It is important where you dwell in life, and 2) you are a citizen of heaven. By the blood of Jesus, you can dwell in the holy of holies, even though you live here on this earth.

Now let's see what Psalm 91:1-4 AMP says:

> He who dwells in the secret place of the Most High
> shall remain stable and fixed under the shadow of
> the Almighty [Whose power no foe can withstand].
> I will say of the Lord, He is my Refuge and my
> Fortress, my God; on Him I lean and rely, and in
> Him I [confidently] trust! For [then] He will deliver
> you from the snare of the fowler and from the
> deadly pestilence. [Then] He will cover you with
> His pinions, and under His wings shall you trust
> and find refuge; His truth and His faithfulness are a
> shield and a buckler.

Notice that Psalm 91 is totally conditional. Two conditions are given in verses 1-2 that must be met before the rest of the verses can be claimed. The first one is that you must dwell in the secret place of God.

The problem is, most Christians don't know how to dwell in the secret place. They think it's a nice phrase, but aren't sure what it means. *Maybe we dwell in the secret place when we pray or go to church,* they think. *But that just isn't so 100 percent of the time.*

However, dwelling in the secret place is a totally reachable goal. All these terms are talking about the same place, a secret place reserved only for God's people. The devil can't get in there. In the secret place of the Most High, you can live safe, healed and protected, abiding continually in the presence of God.

The second condition that must be fulfilled in order to enjoy the benefits of Psalm 91 is that you have to *say* something: "I will *say* of the Lord, He is my Refuge and my Fortress... in Him I [confidently] trust!" (verse 2 AMP). Again, you can see the important role of the words you speak. You have to *say*, "Lord, You are my refuge. I confidently trust You with my life and with my children!"

Once you meet these two conditions, all the other promises of protection in Psalm 91 are yours to claim for your family. Let's read on:

> You shall not be afraid of the terror of the night, nor of the arrow (the evil plots and slanders of the wicked) that flies by day, nor of the pestilence that stalks in darkness, nor of the destruction and sudden death that surprise and lay waste at noonday (verses 5-6 AMP).

These verses talk about the evil plots and slanders of the wicked and the destruction and sudden death that surprises and lays waste at noonday. That sounds like the kinds of things we hear about on the news every night. But it doesn't matter what kinds of evil plots the devil tries against you or your children; his strategies can't prosper. As verse 5 AMP says, "You shall not be afraid of the terror of the night."

That sounds like the covenant man we talked about earlier. He does not fear evil tidings because his heart is fixed on God and His Word.

Now look at verses 7-8 AMP:

> A thousand may fall at your side, and ten thousand at your right hand, but it shall not come near you. Only a spectator shall you be [yourself inaccessible in the secret place of the Most High] as you witness the reward of the wicked.

You are inaccessible to the enemy's strategies when you live in the secret place of the Most High.

Jesus entered the secret place of the Most High, the holy of holies, by His own blood. Our access there is by His blood as well. In that secret place, you and your children are inaccessible to the enemy "because you have made the Lord your refuge, and the Most High your dwelling place" (verse 9 AMP).

Now you can see why Psalm 91 hasn't been fulfilled in many Christians' lives. They may have read it, quoted it, confessed it and prayed it. But if they haven't done what it tells them to do, they're not eligible to receive God's promise of protection for their families.

When the Lord first taught me how to fulfill His conditions so I could receive the promises contained in these verses, I felt like He had given me a very precious gift. As a mother, I so appreciated that gift because now I can be absolutely certain that my family is protected by the blood of Jesus.

I am so thrilled to know that! It doesn't matter what God asks me to do, I can do it boldly because I know He's going to protect my family and me.

I know God will protect your family, too, if you'll just act on these truths. I suggest you read this Psalm to your children every day so its promise of protection can be rooted deeply in their hearts. As you read it, put their names in the verses. Make it personal to them.

You and your children can be safe and secure, no matter what is going on around you. Your part is to dwell in the secret place of the Most High and to speak forth your trust in the Lord. As you do, God will be your family's Refuge and Fortress in every situation. Don't ever let the devil talk you out of that.

Finally, let me plant one more scripture in your heart to build your faith in God's protecting power. Psalm 33:18-19 AMP says, "Behold, the Lord's eye is upon those who fear Him [who revere and worship Him with awe], who wait for Him and hope in His mercy and loving-kindness, to deliver them from death and keep them alive in famine."

It's all through the Word: You and your family can be protected and delivered if you will just receive and appropriate God's promise of protection. Your children can live in that supernatural protection 24 hours a day. You can have what the Word says you can have.

Just live each day the way God intends for you to live— covered in the blood of Jesus, clothed in His righteousness, endowed with His wisdom and abiding in His presence. From your position before the throne of grace, plead the blood of Jesus over yourself, your spouse and your children with the absolute, utter certainty God will keep them safe.

Then, with the words of your mouth, boldly declare your faith in the blood of Jesus:

> "Although we live in a world that is overflowing
> with judgment and sin, we will find only peace,
> protection and abundant grace wherever we go.
> No weapon formed against us shall prosper, for
> the blood of Jesus delivers us from evil and pro-
> tects us from all harm!"

As you pray the following prayer, remember to pray the same over yourself and your spouse. In fact, I include my grandmother in our daily prayer. She's protected by the blood too!

Begin to build the habit of praying like this every day. Ask the Lord to remind you and help you. He will. You may forget sometimes, but keep on. You'll begin to build your covenant on the inside of you. Ask the Lord to never allow you to let these things slip.

You and your family will live your lives from the holy of holies—protected, secure, safe and in His peace.

Prayer of Protection for Your Family

Father, I thank You for Your covenant promise of protection. Right now I call on the covenant I have with You and plead the blood of Jesus over my husband/wife, my children and myself.

Angels, I charge you to watch over my family and me to protect us, for we are walking in the footsteps of Jesus. Go before us, behind us, beside us and all the way around us. Keep us from calamity, evil and misfortune. (I name all of our names to the Lord.)

No evil will befall my family in the Name of Jesus! No weapon formed against them will prosper, and every lying tongue that rises up against them I do condemn, for this is my heritage as a servant of the Lord.

I thank You, Father, that great is the peace of my children. Their righteousness is of You. They don't walk in theirown righteousness, but in Your righteousness by the blood of Jesus. I thank You for that, Lord. They will not get off track in life, none of their steps shall slide (Psalm 37:31), for Your Holy Spirit will guide them every step of the way.

Father, Your Word says that we, Your sheep, know Your voice. It says You will show us things to come. It says the voice of Your Spirit will come to us and say, *This is the way; walk in it.* I stand on these promises, Lord, and ask that You teach us to hear Your voice. Help us recognize when You are speaking to us, and we will obey.

Now I stand in Your holy of holies and open my spirit to receive the wisdom You have made available to me. I put myself in a position to hear and receive instruction from You. I enter the secret place of the Most High by the blood of the Lamb, and I purpose to live my life in Your presence.

I thank You that You are faithful to Your Word, Father. I thank You that what You say is certain and sure. When You say You will deliver us, we can rely on that promise. So right now I receive Your supernatural protection and deliverance for my family and me in Jesus' Name. Amen.

Prayer for Salvation and Baptism in the Holy Spirit

Heavenly Father, I come to You in the Name of Jesus. Your Word says, "Whosoever shall call on the name of the Lord shall be saved" (Acts 2:21). I am calling on You. I pray and ask Jesus to come into my heart and be Lord over my life according to Romans 10:9-10: "If thou shalt confess with thy mouth the Lord Jesus, and shalt believe in thine heart that God hath raised him from the dead, thou shalt be saved. For with the heart man believeth unto righteousness; and with the mouth confession is made unto salvation." I do that now. I confess that Jesus is Lord, and I believe in my heart that God raised Him from the dead. I repent of sin. I renounce it. I renounce the devil and everything he stands for. Jesus is my Lord.

I am now reborn! I am a Christian—a child of Almighty God! I am saved! You also said in Your Word, "If ye then, being evil, know how to give good gifts unto your children: HOW MUCH MORE shall your heavenly Father give the Holy Spirit to them that ask him?" (Luke 11:13). I'm also asking You to fill me with the Holy Spirit. Holy Spirit, rise up within me as I praise God. I fully expect to speak with other tongues as You give me the utterance (Acts 2:4). In Jesus' Name. Amen!

Begin to praise God for filling you with the Holy Spirit. Speak those words and syllables you receive—not in your own language, but the language given to you by the Holy Spirit. You have to use your own voice. God will not force you to speak. Don't be concerned with how it sounds. It is a heavenly language!

Continue with the blessing God has given you and pray in the spirit every day.

You are a born-again, Spirit-filled believer. You'll never be the same!

Find a good church that boldly preaches God's Word and obeys it. Become part of a church family who will love and care for you as you love and care for them.

We need to be connected to each other. It increases our strength in God. It's God's plan for us.

Make it a habit to watch the Believer's Voice of Victory Network and become a doer of the Word, who is blessed in his doing (James 1:22-25).

About the Author
Kellie Copeland

Kellie Copeland is passionate about drawing people of all ages into a growing, personal, and powerful relationship with Jesus Christ. She has seen her passion become a reality through teaching, movies and music.

Whether she is speaking at churches or conferences, Kellie continues to impact generations of children and adults worldwide with the simple message of living the victorious, abundant life in Jesus.

Also known as Commander Kellie, she teaches children how to experience the extraordinary things of God. This has been made possible through Superkid Academy's children's church curriculum and various children's products.

Thankful for the faithful example set by her parents, Kenneth and Gloria Copeland, she partners in sharing the uncompromised word with integrity and love at Kenneth Copeland Ministries in Fort Worth, TX.

Kellie is the mother of 6 amazing children: Rachel and Caleb, Lyndsey, Jenny, Max, and Emily. She has the immeasurable joy of being "Grandmommy" to Rachel and Caleb's two beautiful children, Kenneth and Kate.

Believer's Voice of VICTORY

When The LORD first spoke to Kenneth and Gloria Copeland about starting the *Believer's Voice of Victory* magazine...

He said: *This is your seed. Give it to everyone who ever responds to your ministry, and don't ever allow anyone to pay for a subscription!*

For more than 50 years, it has been the joy of Kenneth Copeland Ministries to bring the good news to believers. Readers enjoy teaching from ministers who write from lives of living contact with God, and testimonies from believers experiencing victory through God's Word in their everyday lives.

Today, the *BVOV* magazine is mailed monthly, bringing encouragement and blessing to believers around the world. Many even use it as a ministry tool, passing it on to others who desire to know Jesus and grow in their faith!

Request your FREE subscription to the *Believer's Voice of Victory* magazine today!

Go to **freevictory.com** to subscribe online, or call us at **1-800-600-7395** (U.S. only) or **+1-817-852-6000**.

We're Here for You!®

Your growth in God's WORD and victory in Jesus are at the very center of our hearts. In every way God has equipped us, we will help you deal with th issues facing you, so you can be the **victorious overcomer** He has planned f you to be.

The mission of Kenneth Copeland Ministries is about all of us growing and going together. Our prayer is that you will take full advantage of all The LORD has given us to share with you.

Wherever you are in the world, you can watch the *Believer's Voice of Victory* broadcast on television (check your local listings), the Internet at kcm.org o on our digital Roku channel.

Our website, **kcm.org,** gives you access to every resource we've developed for your victory. And, you can find contact information for our international offices in Africa, Australia, Canada, Europe, Ukraine and our headquarters i the United States.

Each office is staffed with devoted men and women, ready to serve and pray wi you. You can contact the worldwide office nearest you for assistance, and you ca call us for prayer at our U.S. number, 1-817-852-6000, seven days a week!

We encourage you to connect with us often and let us be part of your everyday walk of faith!

Jesus Is LORD!

Kenneth & Gloria Copeland

Kenneth and Gloria Copeland